Using Literature with Young Children

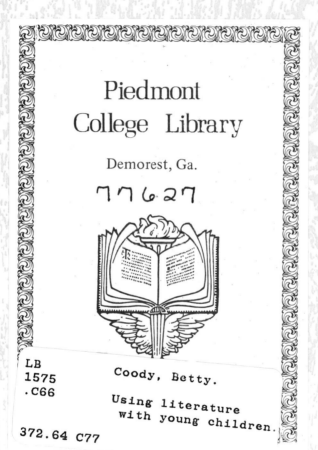

Using Literature with Young Children

BETTY COODY, Lamar University, Beaumont, Texas

WM. C. BROWN COMPANY PUBLISHERS
Dubuque, Iowa

Consulting Editor

Joseph Frost
University of Texas, Austin

Library of Congress Catalog Card Number: 73—76358

ISBN 0—697 06207—4

Fourth Printing, 1976

Printed in the United States of America

2/17/77 Pel. 3.95

To my
Husband

Contents

FOREWORD xi
PREFACE xiii

1

"Read It Again": Books for Reading Aloud 1
TYPES OF LITERATURE FOR YOUNG CHILDREN 2
THE LIBRARY CENTER 6
CHILDREN AS LIBRARIANS 7
THE TEACHER'S READING RECORD 8
THE CHILDREN'S READING RECORD 8
READING ALOUD 9
FOLLOW-UP DISCUSSION 11
QUESTION TYPES 11
BOOKS MADE BY CHILDREN 12
THE PEOPLE WHO MAKE A BOOK 13
THE PARTS OF A BOOK 14
Children's Books for Reading Aloud 15
Bibliography 20

2

"Once Upon a Time": Literature for Storytelling 21
TELLING FOLK TALES TO CHILDREN 24
THE STORYTELLER 25
SELECTING THE STORY 26
PREPARING THE STORY 28
CREATING A CLIMATE 29
SETTING THE TIME 31
BARRIERS TO GOOD STORYTELLING 33
USING VISUAL AIDS 34

Children's Books for Storytelling 39
Bibliography 41

3

"Let's Act It Out": Literature for Dramatization **42**
DRAMATIC PLAY 43
PANTOMIME 45
CREATIVE DRAMATICS 46
PUPPETRY 47
PUPPETRY AND CHILDREN'S LITERATURE 50
PUPPET TYPES 51
PUPPET CONSTRUCTION 52
Children's Books for Dramatization 56
Bibliography 59

4

"Talk Written Down—And More": Books and the Language Experience **60**
EXPERIENCE CHARTS 65
COMPOSING THE EXPERIENCE CHART 67
SOURCES OF EXPERIENCES 67
BOOKS AND THE LANGUAGE EXPERIENCE 69
CHART MAKING 70
ILLUSTRATING THE EXPERIENCE CHART 71
USING THE EXPERIENCE CHART 72
CREATIVE WRITING AND THE LANGUAGE EXPERIENCE 75
THE TEACHER OF CREATIVE WRITING 76
LITERATURE AND CREATIVE WRITING 77
Children's Books for Language Experiences 79
Bibliography 80

5

"Every Young Child is an Artist": Books that Lead to Art Experiences **82**
MURAL MAKING 84
FRIEZE CONSTRUCTION 85
COLLAGE 87
MOSAIC 88
MONTAGE 89
EASEL PAINTING 89
STUDYING THE ART IN CHILDREN'S BOOKS 90
THE CALDECOTT MEDAL 91
Children's Books for Art Experiences 93
Bibliography 96

6

"Better Homes and Kindergartens Cookbook": Books that Lead to Cooking Experiences **97**
HINTS TO THE TEACHER 100
THE POPPY SEED CAKES 101

BLUEBERRIES FOR SAL 103
CHICKEN SOUP WITH RICE 105
BREAD AND JAM FOR FRANCIS 106
THE THANKSGIVING STORY 108
THE DUCHESS BAKES A CAKE 110
THE GINGERBREAD MAN 111
JOURNEY CAKE, HO! 114
STONE SOUP 116
NAIL SOUP 118
THE CARROT SEED 119
THE EGG TREE 121
RAIN MAKES APPLESAUCE 122
WHITE SNOW BRIGHT SNOW 124

7

"Know Thyself": Books for Bibliotherapy **127**
THE BASIC NEEDS 131
Children's Books for Bibliotherapy 137
Bibliography 141

8

"Can You Suggest a Book?": Helping Parents in the Selection and Use of Children's Books **143**
BOOKS AND CONCEPT DEVELOPMENT 146
HOW PARENTS CAN HELP 150
HOW TEACHERS CAN HELP 153
Children's Books for Family Enjoyment 154
Bibliography 157

A

The Caldecott Award Book **159**

B

Directions for a "School-made" Incubator **161**

C

Publisher Index **162**

INDEX 165

Foreword

During the present period of reemphasis upon the development of young children a wide variety of educational patterns are available for promoting literacy. National television programs seek this end through bombardment of the young child with repititious symbols and sounds. The child himself is cast in a passive role—he need not move or engage in mental, social or affective reactions. Ready-made materials are now available for the adult who wishes to "increase the child's I.Q." But the child is infinitely more than an I.Q. He is a feeling, striving, growing *individual* whose multifaceted development is of a piece, integrated and interdependent. Among the alternatives for building literacy and its bases while concurrently promoting positive social and affective development, none is more powerful than literature for children.

This concise book is a resource gold mine for adults working with young children. Professor Coody, working from extensive personal experiences with literature and children, presents a wide sampling of the best literature content and practice and she does this in lucid, concise fashion. Between the initial and closing chapters, "Books for Reading Aloud," and "Books that Help to Meet the Basic Needs of Early Childhood," the aspiring teacher will find direct, "how-to-do-it" suggestions for using literature in imaginative ways. Throughout this book the child is active—reacting, exploring, and assisted in grasping the initiative to extend his creative powers through rhythmic language, universal themes, and the arts.

I am delighted to commend this work to teachers and to other adults with responsibilities for young children. The content will surely enrich the living of those who seek applications in practice.

Joe L. Frost

Preface

This book provides prospective teachers with an introduction to some of the best books available for use with young children from one to eight years of age. It offers an extensive literature program for children both at home and at school, with explicit directions that adults can employ in helping young children become deeply involved with books. Many books have been published in which children's literature is analyzed and critiqued, but this book is unique in that it concentrates solely on literature for early childhood and provides a methodology of teaching literature to young children with their special needs and interests.

In addition, it can be used as a supplementary textbook for introductory courses in early childhood education, as well as courses in children's literature, language arts, and reading.

For those students who wish to do further reading on the various themes presented, a bibliography and suggested readings are included at the end of each chapter. Also given at the end of each chapter is an annotated bibliography of children's books which can be used as an aid in the study, selection and purchase of books.

I wish to express my gratitude to the many people who helped in the preparation of this manuscript. William Mayette spent many hours in making my photography look less amateurish. Mary Langston and Judy Potter of the Tyrell Public Library made their excellent children's collection available and offered valuable suggestions. Martha Knight served as my research assistant and tracked down elusive references for many months. Faye Briggs did an outstanding job in typing the complete manuscript. My husband knows how much I have relied on his help and encouragement. He took many of the pictures used to illustrate the book, and assisted in countless other ways. I deeply appreciate the editorial assistance of Dr. Joe Frost. His suggestions always reflected a concern for young children and their education. I am indebted to the teachers in public and private schools who allowed me to observe their literature program in action and to take pictures of the children. A special debt of gratitude is owed to the students in my college classes. They have taught me so many things over the years, and their ideas are reflected throughout this book.

Betty Coody

1

"Read It Again": Books for Reading Aloud

Too many of today's children fail in school, and poor reading lies at the heart of most such failures. Of those children who are fortunate enough to learn the basic skills of reading, many come to dislike the process so much that they seldom read a book outside the classroom. Often reading has been taught in such a heavy-handed manner that children have not had the privilege of reading books for sheer pleasure or to satisfy personal needs and interests. And unless wholesome attitudes toward books and reading are developed when a child is still quite young, it is extremely doubtful that he will ever become a reading adult.

Many concerned and knowledgeable educators have felt for some time that over-reliance on textbook lessons and workbook exercises in the teaching of beginning reading is largely responsible for the high rate of reading failure and for the obvious lack of enthusiasm toward literature that appears in the upper grades. Fortunately, in the past few years there has been a promising trend toward "library centered" reading programs—programs in which trade books of all kinds are used to whet the appetites of young children and to leave with them a lasting desire to read. Abraham

Shumsky gives a convincing argument for reading readiness programs based on children's experiences with literature:

> . . . Reading readiness should be equated with a rich program aiming at promoting language facility and intellectual curiosity about books and their message. A program of this nature will include discussion, trips, films, listening to literature and poetry books read by the teacher, accompanied by open discussion about them, children's own "reading" of stories by looking at the pictures, children's dictation of stories and poems, science experiments, and experience charts which illustrate to the child the process of transforming ideas into reading matter.[1]

Research findings continue to point up that the early years of a child's life are the critical ones in determining the patterns of social and emotional development. The way a person feels about himself and others, and how he perceives the world in which he finds himself is largely determined during the highly formative years from birth to age eight. And literature—or in many cases the absence of literature—has an important part to play in personality development. As a result of this knowledge, many of our best artists and writers have turned their attention to creating fine books for the youngest children. Beautiful picture books that embody profound philosophies are being published every year. Young children are well able to grapple with such big ideas as "cultural plurality," "interdependence of man," and "environmental control" if they are presented in an interesting way and at the child's level of understanding. As a matter of fact, young children are proving to be our very best philosophers. Perhaps they will be able to find solutions to the problems that plague us.

It is rather ironic that at the time when a child is most influenced by his experiences with books, he is almost completely at the mercy of adult choices. Parents, teachers, librarians, and other adults select the books and decide how they will be used. In the process, too many children are forced to exist on an impoverished literary diet. This is not an argument for young children to be given the privilege of complete self-selection in literature. It is, on the contrary, a plea for parents and teachers to acquaint themselves with the best in children's books and to make use of a variety of experiences that will enhance the enjoyment of literature.

Types of Literature for Young Children

Young children begin to look at reading as a necessary and integral part of their lives when respected adults are skillful at sharing good litera-

1. Abraham Shumsky, *Creative Teaching in the Elementary School* (New York: Appleton-Century-Crofts, 1965), p. 92.

Fig. 1.1. Young children are able to deal with such big ideas as "environmental control." Here they study the world as found within the confines of a hula hoop. (Courtesy of Saint Thomas Episcopal School, College Station, Texas.)

Fig. 1.2. In a study of waste disposal, these children bury orange peels to be dug up later. They plan to observe the effects of decomposition. (Courtesy of Saint Thomas Episcopal School, College Station, Texas.)

ture with them. Parents and teachers should recognize that reading aloud is the means by which the pre-reading child is led into the world of books. Listening to someone read aloud should be considered not only as an indication of reading readiness, but also reading in the fullest sense of the word. The child studies the pictures and follows the story line as the adult unlocks the printed symbols for him. Both are engrossed in the reading process.

In selecting books for reading aloud to young children at home or at school, Leland Jacobs has developed a set of criteria to guide adults:

1. The story should have a fresh well-paced plot.
2. It must have unique individuality.
3. It should contain plausible, direct conversation.
4. It must have well-delineated characters.
5. The story must have an authentic outcome.[2]

2. Leland B. Jacobs, "Children's Experiences in Literature," *Children and the Language Arts,* eds. Virgil E. Herrick and Leland B. Jacobs. (Englewood Cliffs, N. J.: Prentice-Hall, Inc., 1955), p. 194.

Moreover, the adult will be wise to select books having one main plot, a rousing climax, and a fairly predictable outcome. Other features young children prefer in their literature are: action, conflict, heroic characters, and tongue-teasing language. They also want illustrations that are perfectly synchronized with the text.

In choosing books to read aloud to young children, it is necessary to consider the various categories of literature that are recommended for the early childhood library. Since there is seldom enough money to buy all the desired books at one time, a satisfactory plan is to develop priority lists in which certain books are purchased from different classifications until a varied collection has been acquired. Even a small collection can be a well-balanced one. Examples of each type of literature found in the following categories are reviewed at the end of the chapter.

Mother Goose. The humanism, the fun and nonsense, the high adventure, and the rhythmic language of Mother Goose stories have strong appeal for each generation of children. These old folk rhymes have been called the perfect literature for early childhood. As many editions of Mother Goose as the budget will allow should be provided for the classroom. In addition to books, children enjoy puzzles, art prints, pillows, figurines, filmstrips, and other materials that depict their favorite Mother Goose characters.

Alphabet Books. ABC books are used by parents and teachers to entertain children and to familiarize them with letters of the alphabet and the sound that each letter represents. ABC books may be illustrated by means of photographs, realistic paintings, or semi-abstract art. Purchasers of ABC books should make certain that each letter of the alphabet is represented by meaningful objects. Only one or two objects should be presented on each page and the letter should stand out in bold relief.

Counting Books. Counting books are used to present a few basic mathematical concepts and the symbols that represent them. Number books are a necessary part of the early childhood library in that they afford the most enjoyable means of acquainting young children with the language of mathematics.

A counting book should have the same high quality art work that is expected in other kinds of literature for children. Each numeral should have a prominent place on its own page. Shapes and forms used to represent the concept of the numeral should be balanced and spaced on the page in such a way as to avoid clutter and confusion.

Concept Books. Concept books are designed to help young children develop the ability to generalize and conceptualize. Abstract ideas such as size, shape, speed, and weight are presented in graphic, artistic form. Teachers usually find it best to read concept books aloud to small groups or to individual children, and to explain and clarify as they go. Concept books must be chosen with care if they are to coincide with the maturity level of the children.

Machines Personified. Machines personified refers to books in which machines and other inanimate objects are endowed with human qualities by the author and illustrator. The stories are often inspirational in nature since the plot is built around some staggering, overwhelming task to be accomplished by the machine. Success is always realized and the happy ending leaves the reader or listener with a sense of deep satisfaction.

Animal Stories. Most animal stories preferred by the youngest children are of the "talking beast tale" variety. These are stories in which the beasts are more human than animal. They work, play, laugh, cry, make foolish mistakes, and perform acts of kindness and wisdom. Children rank them at the top among stories they prefer to have read again and again. James Moffett explains why an animal story like "The Three Billy Goats Gruff" satisfies a young child's desire for novelty and excitement, while at the same time organizes experience in reassuring and resolving ways:

> An ogre tries to eat up anyone who crosses his bridge to graze on the pleasant slopes beyond. Between us and the attainment of our desires lie frightful dangers that we cannot go around. The smallest billy goat encounters the ogre and persuades him to spare his life in favor of eating the larger goat to come. The second billy goat gets by the same way, and the third tears the ogre apart (into a satisfying number of small pieces). The three goats reach and enjoy the pasture. If you're weak and helpless, a child, you can refer the danger to Mother, who, if she cannot cope with it, can refer it to Daddy. *Some* "big person" will come along who is capable of overcoming the forces of evil and ensuring that you get what you have to have without being destroyed in the process. The small are backed up by the mighty, but you may have to make shift with a stratagem of your own. And you have to play on your size, not deny it.[3]

Talking beast tales are, of course, perfect for storytelling as well as for reading aloud, and can be told with a minimum of memorization.

3. James Moffett, *A Student-Centered Language Arts Curriculum, Grades K-12: A Handbook for Teachers* (Boston: Houghton Mifflin Co., 1968), pp. 117-18.

Humor and Nonsense Books. Books from all classifications may be considered humorous books if they make children laugh. One of the basic needs of all children, as well as adults, is the need for change, and a delightful way to enjoy the therapy that comes with change is to read a book made up of humor and nonsense. If children fail to see the humor in a book, it should be reserved for a later date. Perhaps with more maturity they will be able to enjoy the wit intended by the author. Plenty of humorous books are available, guaranteed to make children laugh. There is no need to dwell on a book beyond their understanding.

Picture Books. Picture books are those in which the pictures play such important roles that the text would be incomplete without them. The favorite picture books of young children are the ones in which the pictures carry the story so well that even a pre-reading child can follow along. The text that is used in a picture book must be read aloud to beginning readers, since the readability level is usually about third grade.

The Caldecott Award is presented each year to "the artist of the most distinguished American picture book for children." The winning book is selected by a special committee of the Children's Services Division of the American Library Association. A complete list of the Caldecott medal books, the artist and publisher of each one, and the year the award was conferred is presented in Appendix A.

Easy-to-Read Books. Books classified as easy-to-read are those that employ a controlled vocabulary of frequently used words. Only a few words are used and they are repeated throughout the text. The print is large and surrounded by ample white space. Pictures are used to help tell the story, and the text embodies a great deal of conversation. All these features are combined to make a book that is entertaining, informational and, above all, easy to read. Any child who can read fluently at the primer level should be able to cope with most of the easy-to-read books.

The Library Center

A book corner containing a variety of books attractively arranged can well become a calm and quiet oasis in a busy classroom. Some teachers set the book center apart with a small rug. Others screen it off with low book shelves or with an enticing bulletin board. A reading table should be provided for the center, and comfortable slipcovered chairs. A child-sized rocking chair is a popular item in the library corner.

A neat, well organized library center is always attractive because the books themselves are works of art, but a few green plants, some choice art prints, and a piece of good sculpture that has child appeal will definitely add to its beauty. Any effort that goes into making the classroom library an inviting spot will pay rich dividends in reading achievement and in reading interest.

Because the library center should be the quietest and most private area in the classroom, it is wise to locate it out of the line of traffic. On the other hand, such a location can cause a lighting problem. To avoid a gloomy, dreary book corner, it may be necessary to provide a table lamp in addition to the traditional classroom lighting.

It is of absolute necessity to display many of the books face out. The spine means nothing to a child who cannot yet read, and very little to a beginning reader. Shelves should be wide and deep enough to hold the over-sized picture books with their covers showing. Book jackets are designed to invite browsing. If the jacket is hidden or removed, the value of its sales appeal is lost. Some books, of course, are displayed flat on the table, others standing in book racks. Some books should be kept in a cabinet to be brought out on special occasions. This is especially true of holiday books, seasonal books, books with limited appeal, and perhaps books held on reserve for use as bibliotherapy.

Children as Librarians

It is advisable to create classroom library committees on a rotating basis so that responsibilities and privileges can be shared in a routine fash-

Figs. 1.3 and 1.4. With a reading loft in the kindergarten classroom, a child who wishes to look at a book in privacy may retreat "far from the madding crowd," but not *too* far. The reading loft should be carpeted, well-lighted, and restricted to a few children at a time. A reading loft only supplements the library center in the room. It should not replace it. (Courtesy of West Orange-Cove Independent School District, Orange, Texas.)

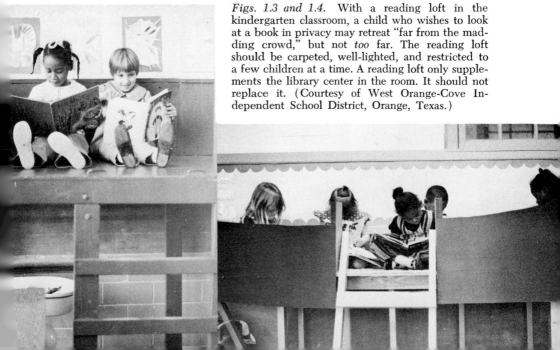

ion. Children appreciate the library center much more if they have had a hand in planning it, arranging it, and in keeping it clean and orderly. It is surprising how well they are able to arrange the books into categories that have meaning for them. They are also quite capable of operating a simple check-out system for books that are to be taken home. Such a program cannot operate successfully without careful planning and continuous supervision on the teacher's part. The teacher should be aware that attitudes and feelings about books and reading are being developed during the early years of a child's schooling, and that those attitudes and feelings will remain with him throughout life.

The Teacher's Reading Record

Most teachers feel the need to keep a running record of the books a child selects to read (or takes out for someone to read to him). This is a sound practice. Such a list can serve as ready material for the parent-teacher conference, and offers a graphic way to show the child's level of reading and his interest in certain subjects. It may also serve to tell the teacher how much silent reading practice a student is getting. In many ways a list of self-selected trade books read by a child provides a better picture of reading growth than the traditional check list of basal textbooks completed.

The Children's Reading Record

The value of the reading record that a child keeps for himself cannot be overestimated. As he completes a book, the child writes the title on a small card and files it in his personal and private pocket on a large teacher-made chart. The card pack mounts up until the end of a semester, at which time it can be taken home with a letter of explanation to parents. Such a report is good news to parents and is one way a young child can be shown that he is making progress.

Some perceptive teachers employ the three-way conference method in meeting with parents, which includes the child. In such cases, the child's personal reading record gives him material in hand to make a worthy contribution as he talks with his parents and his teacher.

In any system of record keeping, there should be no competition among students as to the number of books read. No rewards or reprimands are given in connection with the reading record. The record itself, however, does serve as motivation toward more reading. It is a dignified way in which a child can compete with his own past record. Some teachers change the color of the cards each month. In this way a child can tell at a

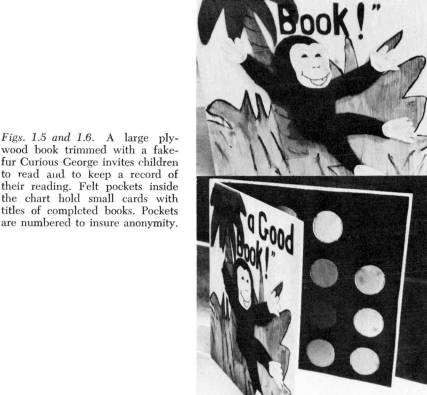

Figs. 1.5 and 1.6. A large plywood book trimmed with a fake-fur Curious George invites children to read and to keep a record of their reading. Felt pockets inside the chart hold small cards with titles of completed books. Pockets are numbered to insure anonymity.

glance if he has read as many books in May as he did in April. Again, the record is solely for the child's information and perhaps as an indicator to the teacher. It should never be used as a basis for assigning a grade.

Reading Aloud

Adjacent to the library center a carpeted area should be set aside for gathering the children together in an intimate story circle. The teacher can then sit at the edge of the circle on a low chair and hold the picture book at the eye level of the children. She must of course, master the art of reading from the side so that the children are able to see the illustrations at all times.

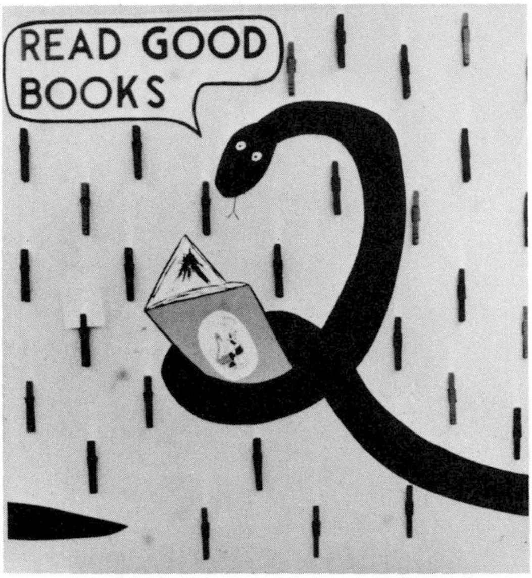

Fig. 1.7. Crictor encourages children to read, and serves as an example by reading about himself. Students keep a record of books completed by clipping small cards to clothes pins. The chart is made of thin wood.

Fig. 1.8. A pet monkey, a toy monkey, and the book *Curious George* are combined to enrich the child's background of experiences. (Courtesy of South Park Independent School District, Beaumont, Texas.)

If the story is to be read with feeling and enjoyment, it should be selected and prepared in advance. Obviously, the teacher should choose only those stories she enjoys, since boredom with a story will always be transmitted to the listeners. The story should be read in a well-modulated voice that does not over dramatize the conversational parts. Leave something to the imagination of children.

Follow-up Discussion

No harm is done to the story if the reader pauses briefly to define a word or point out a comparison, but any lengthy discussion should be reserved until the story is ended. Children readily become accustomed to this routine and are willing to hold most of their questions in abeyance.

Not every book will be discussed on completion. Some stories are so moving that any comment would be superfluous. But follow-up discussion can be a rich learning experience. It can improve comprehension and heighten the appreciation of a story. The art of asking provocative questions about a piece of literature is an important teaching skill and can easily be mastered with a little practice. In using the questioning method, the teacher should never become so preoccupied with the upcoming question that she fails to listen to the responses of children. In fact, most questions should spring naturally from the children's reactions to the book.

Question Types

In order to illustrate how questioning may proceed from surface questions to the higher-level questioning that calls for personal involvement, the story, *Snipp, Snapp, Snurr and the Red Shoes* by Maj Lindman will serve as example.[4] It is a tale of three small boys who find odd jobs and earn enough money to buy their mother a pair of birthday shoes. The story lends itself well to class discussion.

Recognition and Recall

What were the names of the boys?
What kind of clothing did they wear?
How did their clothes change color?
What kind of pet did they have?
What did they tell Mother about their day?

4. Maj Lindman, *Snipp, Snapp, Snurr and the Red Shoes* (Chicago: Albert Whitman & Co., 1936).

Demonstration of Skill

Could you show how Snipp painted the fence?
Could you show how Snapp cleaned the chimney?
Could you show how Snurr worked in the flour mill?
How would you earn money for a gift? Act it out.

Comprehension and Analysis

Why did they have to put their money together to buy the gift?
Why didn't they each buy something different?
Why did the boys ask Mother if she wanted a red wagon, or a train, or a pony?
Why did she *not* want these things?
Why did they leave home to earn the money?
Why were they in such a hurry to find jobs?

Synthesis

What would have happened if the man had sold the shoes to someone else?
What if the shoes had been too small?

Opinion

How do you suppose they knew Mother's shoe size?
How do you think Mother liked the shoes?

Attitudes and Values

How do you feel when you earn money?
Did you ever spend all your money on another person?
How did it feel when you did that?

Books Made by Children

Once a child has made a book of his own, he has a higher regard for all books. Children usually begin making books of many kinds during nursery school and kindergarten. At first they may simply paste pictures cut from magazines and catalogues into categories such as "red" and "blue," or "fruits" and "vegetables," or boys" and "girls." Later, they may talk about their own art work as the teacher records their comments under the picture in manuscript writing. In this way, each child has composed and illustrated his own story.

Still later, when the children have gained skill in the mechanics of writing, they will be able to write and illustrate their own stories with very little help from the teacher. As the teacher fastens the pages together and labels the cover "Good Stories," the children get a generalized impression of how a book is made. They also have firsthand experience at what it is like to be an author and an illustrator, especially if the teacher takes advantage of the experience to draw a parallel.

Books written, illustrated, and bound by children should be given a prominent place in the library center to be read by the children and checked out for home reading.

Fig. 1.9. This classmade book is a source of pride and enjoyment to the third-graders who wrote it. It is composed of a series of their reactions to *Charlie and the Chocolate Factory* by Roald Dahl. (Courtesy of West Harden Independent School District, Sour Lake, Texas.)

The People Who Make a Book

Young children are keenly interested in news and information about the authors and illustrators of their favorite books. A teacher of six-year-olds explained to the children that an author of her acquaintance was writing a story about a horned lizard he had captured. He had put honey on his wife's clothesline to attract a supply of ants for the horned lizard as he studied it in captivity. When the book was finished, he sent the class an autographed copy. Even though it was an informational book of science, the children read it over and over again and frequently requested that it be read aloud at story time.

In addition to the author and illustrator, young children can also understand something about the publisher of a book. The name of the publishing company can be pointed out to them in all the places it normally appears in a book. Occasionally they are interested in the city where the publishing firm is located. The function of the publisher as manufacturer, advertiser, and bookseller is better understood if the class is given the privilege of selecting a book from a catalogue and then ordering it directly from the publisher. One seven-year-old was heard to comment, "All of Dr. Seuss's books come from Random House."

The Parts of a Book

Young children are interested in the parts of a book in direct ratio to the teacher's interest in the way a book is put together. The following parts are those most often discussed and examined in the early years of school.

The *jacket* is the colorful paper cover that folds around the outside of the book. It serves as eye appeal to the prospective reader, and as protection for the book.

The flaps are the parts of the jacket that fold inside the front and back covers of the book. The front flap contains a brief summary of the book's contents. Children like calling the summary by its proper name, the "blurb." The back flap usually contains essential information about the author and illustrator, and is sometimes called the "continuation of the blurb." (If publishers could see the way boys and girls pore over a picture of their favorite author or illustrator, they would undoubtdly make certain that every back flap contained such photographs.)

The *book cover,* the outside covering of the book, is composed of heavy cardboard covered with paper or cloth. Similar covers can easily be constructed for child-made books by covering cardboard with contact paper.

The *end papers* are those papers pasted in the front and back of a book to cover up the rough edges of the binding. The end papers are often decorated in such a way that they offer a glimpse into the contents of the book. In *Blueberries for Sal,* by Robert McCloskey, the end papers show Sal "helping" her mother can blueberries for the winter. The illustration is said to be an authentic representation of the kitchen in McClosky's boyhood home in Maine. It probably has as much socio-cultural content for the young child as any one picture could possess.

The *title page* is the first printed page in a book. It carries the name of the author, illustrator, and publisher. The title page is important to children only if they have been given an understanding of who these three people are and their special role in the creation of a book.

The *spine* of a book is the part of a book that is visible when the book is shelved. It is the central support or the "backbone" of a book. The spine usually carries the title of the book, last name of the author, and the name of the publisher. A pre-reading child should not be expected to rely on the spine for selecting a book since it contains no identifying picture of any kind. The spine is, however, extremely important to the child who can read since most libraries shelve books with only the spine showing.

In conclusion, whether or not young children gain the maximum benefit from a home or classroom collection will depend almost entirely on the amount of effort expended by parents, teachers, and other significant adults.

Reading aloud to young children at home can bring about some of the most memorable family occasions, while routine reading aloud at school has the power to improve attitudes toward reading and toward school in general. E. Paul Torrance has written: "It now seems possible that many things can be learned in creative ways more economically and effectively than by authority."[5] Reading aloud from quality literature is one of the creative ways to teach young children.

CHILDREN'S BOOKS FOR READING ALOUD

Mother Goose Books

Book of Nursery and Mother Goose Rhymes, compiled and illustrated by Marguerite de Angeli. Garden City, N. Y.: Doubleday & Co., Inc., 1953. Soft, delicate black and white drawings interspersed with mellow pastel paintings make this fine edition a work of art. Contains 376 of the most popular rhymes.

Mother Goose, compiled and illustrated by Tasha Tudor. New York: Henry Z. Walck, Inc., 1944. Quaint, old-fashioned costumes give Tasha Tudor's Mother Goose characters added charm. Contains seventy-seven well-known verses.

The Real Mother Goose, illustrated by Blanche Fisher Wright with introduction by May Hill Arbuthnot. Chicago: Rand McNally & Co., 1944. An edition consistently popular with children for over fifty years. Contains an interesting account of the origins of Mother Goose.

The Tall Book of Mother Goose, compiled and illustrated by Feodor Rojankovsky. New York: Harper & Row, Publishers, 1942. Humorous, cartoon-like illustrations and the tall shape of the book make this edition unique among the many versions of Mother Goose.

The Tenggren Mother Goose, compiled and illustrated by Gustaf Tenggren. Boston: Little, Brown & Co., 1940. A beautifully illustrated edition with many

5. E. Paul Torrance, *Creativity* (Washington, D. C.: The National Education Association, 1963), p. 3.

small pictures sprinkled over every page for young children to find and study.

Alphabet Books

ABC, An Alphabet Book, photographed by Thomas Matthiesen. New York: Platt & Munk, Publishers, 1966. A beautiful photograph in full color of a well known object represents each letter of the alphabet. An excellent transition from concrete objects to semi-abstract art.

The ABC Bunny, by Wanda Gág. New York: Coward-McCann, Inc., 1933. Soft black and white drawings illustrate the adventures of a small bunny. Each letter of the alphabet stands out in bright red against a white background. A favorite ABC book of children for many years.

First ABC, written by Nancy Larrick and illustrated by René Martin. New York: Platt & Munk, Publishers, 1965. Each double page contains one large illustration with a brief, factual story about the picture. Each story is accompanied by the appropriate letter in both upper and lower case. Excellent suggestions for ways to use the book are presented for benefit of parents and teachers.

In a Pumpkin Shell, by Joan Walsh Anglund. New York: Harcourt Brace Jovanovich, Inc., 1960. A Mother Goose ABC book in which each nursery rhyme is preceded by a letter of the alphabet and one key word from the verse that begins with the letter shown. Illustrations are rich in detail.

The Marcel Marceau Alphabet Book, written by George Mendoza and photographed by Milton H. Green. Garden City, N. Y.: Doubleday & Co., Inc., 1970. Marcel Marceau, the world's greatest pantomimist, bends his lithe body into the characterization of a word representing each letter of the alphabet. Superb photographs of Marceau completely surrounded by empty white space. Only the letter of the alphabet is shown in color.

Peter Piper's Alphabet, illustrated by Marcia Brown. New York: Charles Scribner's Sons, 1959. Sounds of the alphabet are represented by famous old tongue-twisting nonsense rhymes. The pictures are filled with fun and foolishness to be enjoyed by children and adults alike.

Counting Books

My First Counting Book, written by Lilian Moore and illustrated by Garth Williams. New York: Simon & Schuster, 1956. A sturdy counting book for beginners. Each number to ten is represented by a familiar plant or animal. Complete review included at the end of the book.

Still Another Number Book, by Seymour Chwast and Martin Stephen Moskof. New York: McGraw-Hill Book Co., 1971. A new number book with a contemporary look. It proceeds from one ship to ten jugglers and then reverses itself to go from ten jugglers down to one ship. Fun for the entire family.

The Twelve Days of Christmas, illustrated by Ilonka Karaz. New York: Harper & Row, Publishers, 1949. The ordinal numbers through "twelfth" are reviewed, beginning with the first day of Christmas and a partridge in a pear tree. The gifts accumulate up to the last page where all are shown in sequential order. The book contains sheet music to the old folk song.

1 is One, by Tasha Tudor. New York: Henry Z. Walck, Inc., 1956. A counting book that is also a book of art. Plants and animals, flowers and fruit decorate the pages in delicate pastel colors or in soft black and white.

Concept Books

We Read A to Z, by Donald Crews. New York: Harper & Row, Publishers, 1967. An alphabet book that teaches concepts and ideas. ("A is for almost. Z is for zigzag.") Each letter of the alphabet is used to introduce a concept; each concept is illustrated with a colorful design. A book that is as fascinating to adults as it is to children.

The Adventures of Three Colors, by Annette Tison and Talus Taylor. Cleveland, Ohio: World Publishing Co., 1971. Explanation of how a rainbow is formed by the division of white light into many colors. As Herbie paints with the three primary colors he has seen in the rainbow, he discovers he can make other colors. Clever overlays show how the primary colors combine to form secondary colors and finally tertiary colors.

Machines Personified

The Little Engine that Could, by Watty Piper. New York: Platt & Munk, Publishers, 1955. A favorite story about a little engine with a difficult task to accomplish. "I think I can, I think I can" has helped many a child over a high hurdle.

Little Toot, by Hardie Gramatky, New York: G. P. Putnam's Sons, 1939. The story of a mischievous little tugboat who refuses to accept the responsibility of tugboat duties. The other boats have to do his share of the work until Little Toot finally proves his worth by courageous action in a dangerous crisis.

Little Toot on the Thames, by Hardie Gramatky. New York: G. P. Putnam's Sons, 1965. A sequel written on the twenty-fifth anniversary of *Little Toot.* Little Toot is accidentally towed to England by a huge tramp steamer and winds up in the Thames River. After many disgraces and successes, Little Toot is escorted back home by the good ship Queen Elizabeth.

Mike Mulligan and His Steam Shovel, written and illustrated by Virginia Lee Burton. Boston: Houghton Mifflin Co., 1939. Mary Anne is a steam shovel with personality who digs her way into a deep hole and is unable to get out again. The ending is humorous and satisfying.

Animal Stories

Curious George, by Hans A. Rey. Boston: Houghton Mifflin Co., 1941. This curious little monkey is very much like a child as he explores and examines his environment. His curiosity leads him into trouble, but his friend in the yellow hat always gets him out again. The first in a series of books about Curious George.

Harry the Dirty Dog, written by Gene Zion and illustrated by Margaret B. Graham. New York: Harper & Row, Publishers, 1956. The story of a dog who gets so dirty that he is unrecognizable, and finds that soap and water are important to him after all.

How, Hippo!, written and illustrated by Marcia Brown. New York: Charles Scribner's Sons, 1969. An entertaining tale of how a mother hippopotamus teaches her baby hippo to protect himself from enemies by making him learn certain grunts and roars. Beautifully illustrated by means of a woodcut technique.

The Little Rabbit Who Wanted Red Wings, by Carolyn Sherwin Bailey. New York: Platt & Munk, Publishers, 1951. On making a wish at the wishing pond, Little White Rabbit finds he can have long red wings. After losing his friends and family because no one recognizes him, he decides it is better for him to be just a little white rabbit. He promises he will never again wish to be anything but what he really is.

Millions of Cats, by Wanda Gág, New York: Coward-McCann, Inc., 1928. Out of the millions of cats, only one was humble and modest, but that one turns out to be the most beautiful and lovable of all. A modern folk tale illustrated with black and white drawings.

The Secret Hiding Place, by Rainey Bennett. Cleveland, Ohio: World Publishing Co., 1960. Little Hippo attempts to find his own secret hiding place where he can be alone. Eventually, he finds a high cliff that makes a perfect hiding place. He is able to get away from the herd of hippos and yet keep them safely in sight.

The Story of Ferdinand, written by Munro Leaf and illustrated by Robert Lawson. New York: The Viking Press, 1936. All the other bulls wanted to fight more than anything else. But not Ferdinand. He just wanted to sit quietly under the cork tree and smell the flowers. "His mother saw that he was not lonesome, and because she was an understanding mother, even though she was a cow, she let him just sit there and be happy." A gentle satire on bullfighting and a tongue-in-cheek account of a nonconforming individual.

Humor and Nonsense

Crictor, by Tomi Ungerer. New York: Harper & Row, Publishers, 1968. As a birthday gift, Madame Louise Bodot receives a boa constrictor from her son who is studying reptiles in Africa. Crictor makes a good pet and rescues his mistress from a burglar. Some letters of the alphabet and the numerals through eight are reviewed as Crictor coils his body into various shapes for the amusement of his friends.

Horton Hatches the Egg, by Dr. Seuss (Theodore Seuss Geisel). New York: Random House, 1940. Dr. Seuss has been called a modern Edward Lear, and Horton is one of his most popular characters. An elephant up in a tree is the kind of humor that appeals to young children. The story has a happy surprise ending.

Johnny Crow's Garden, written and illustrated by Leslie Brooke. New York: Frederick Warne and Co., 1903. The fun and humor in *Johnny Crow's Garden* and its sequels have proven irresistable to children and adults alike for many years. Illustrated with nonsensical but highly artistic drawings in black and white.

Rain Makes Applesauce, written by Julian Sheer and illustrated by Marvin Bileck. New York: Holiday House, 1964. This is a fanciful, imaginative book of silly talk, the kind of silly talk children like to create for themselves. The illustrations are intricate and filled with humorous detail. There is one bit of realism on each page. In the lower right corner is a sequential story of applesauce from the planting of the seed to the cooking and eating of applesauce.

Sylvester and the Magic Pebble, by William Steig, New York: Simon & Schuster, 1969. Sylvester Duncan is a young donkey who lives with his mother and father at Acorn Road in Oatsdale. What happens to Sylvester when he finds a magic pebble makes for humor and suspense. The illustrations are done in cartoon style and form a perfect complement to the droll text.

Picture Books

Amigo, written by Byrd Baylor Schweitzer and illustrated by Garth Williams. New York: The Macmillan Co., 1963. Francisco, a little Mexican boy, wants a pet dog more than anything, but his parents are too poor to feed another mouth. Instead, Francisco decides to tame a prairie dog. At the same time, a prairie dog is making plans to tame himself a boy. How the two finally become fast friends is told in rhythmic verse much like an American folk song.

Cinderella, illustrated by Marcia Brown, New York: Charles Scribner's Sons, 1954. The author-artist's delicate illustrations help to make this rags-to-riches story a more delightful folk tale than ever. One of our oldest stories of social mobility. A Caldecott Award winner.

Crow Boy, written and illustrated by Taro Yashima, New York: The Viking Press, 1955. Chibi, a young Japanese boy, shows how much he values schooling by "leaving his home for school at sunrise, every day for six long years." He is the only one in his class to be honored for perfect attendance. And yet, Chibi is an outsider, never accepted by his peers until an understanding schoolmaster discovers that he can imitate the voices of crows. Chibi finally attains the status he deserves. Beautiful oriental illustrations.

The Happy Owls, written and illustrated by Celestino Piatti. New York: Atheneum, 1964. The barnyard fowls do nothing but fight and quarrel all day, and they wonder why the owls never seem to fight. On inquiry, the owls explain how they are able to live together in peace. The fowls listen, but understand none of it. They immediately turn back to their quarrelsome ways. The story is illustrated in bold black outlines and bright poster colors. A beautiful book with a subtle message.

The Little Island, written by Golden MacDonald and illustrated by Leonard Weisgard, Garden City, N. Y.: Doubleday & Co., Inc., 1946. The little island is shown as having responsibility to the rest of the world in the same way that a person is a necessary part of the society in which he lives. A Caldecott Award winner.

Easy-to-Read Books

Are You My Mother?, by P. D. Eastman. New York: Random House, 1960. A very funny book for children who are just beginning to read. A baby bird hatches out and cannot find his mother. He does not even know what she looks like; he mistakes a dog, a cow, a cat, a plane, a boat, and a steam shovel for his mother. Uses only one hundred easy-to-read words.

Little Bear's Visit, written by Else Holmelund Minarik and illustrated by Maurice Sendak. New York: Harper & Row, Publishers, 1961. A tale of Little Bear's visit to Grandmother and Grandfather Bear who live in a little house in the woods. One of several easy-to-read books about Little Bear, his family and friends.

BIBLOGRAPHY

Anderson, William, and Groff, Patrick. *A New Look at Children's Literature.* Belmont, Calif.: Wadsworth Publishing Co., Inc., 1972.

Arbuthnot, May Hill. *Children and Books.* 4th ed. Glenview, Ill.: Scott, Foresman and Co., 1972.

Georgiou, Constantine. *Children and Their Literature.* Englewood Cliffs, N. J.: Prentice-Hall, Inc., 1969.

Hollowell, Lillian. *A Book of Children's Literature.* 3rd ed. New York: Holt, Rinehart & Winston, Inc., 1966.

Huck, Charlotte, and Kuhn, Doris Young. *Children's Literature in the Elementary School.* 2nd ed. New York: Holt, Rinehart & Winston, Inc., 1968.

Jacobs, Leland B. "Children's Experiences in Literature." In *Children and the Language Arts.* Edited by Virgil E. Herrick and Leland B. Jacobs. Englewood Cliffs, N. J.: Prentice-Hall, Inc., 1955.

Larrick, Nancy. *A Parent's Guide to Children's Reading.* 3rd ed. New York: Pocket Books, 1969.

———. *A Teacher's Guide to Children's Books.* abridged ed. Columbus, Ohio: Charles E. Merrill Publishers, 1960.

Lindman, Maj. *Snipp, Snapp, Snurr and the Red Shoes.* Chicago: Albert Whitman & Co., 1936.

Meeker, Alice M. *Enjoying Literature with Children.* New York: The Odyssey Press, 1969.

Moffett, James. *A Student-Centered Language Arts Curriculum, Grades K-12: A Handbook for Teachers.* Boston: Houghton Mifflin Co., 1968.

Nelson, Mary Anne. *A Comparative Anthology of Children's Literature.* New York: Holt, Rinehart & Winston, Inc., 1972.

Shumsky, Abraham. *Creative Teaching in the Elementary School.* New York: Appleton-Century-Crofts, 1965.

Torrance, E. Paul. *Creativity.* Washington, D. C.: The National Education Association, 1963.

2

"Once Upon a Time": Literature for Storytelling

The art of storytelling flourished long before there was a written language to record the tales. Men have always gathered to talk over common problems, to ponder on natural phenomena they could not understand, to lavish praise on their heroes, both real and imaginary, to celebrate victories and accomplishments, and to mourn tragic losses.

As people began to travel over longer and longer distances, the stories were carried from one locale to another, changing slightly as each storyteller added embellishments to suit his audience and his own storytelling style. It is believed that folk tales traveled mainly from the Far East to the Middle East and from there to Europe. Finally, the tales were carried from Europe to North and South America.

Today, each country of the world has its own wealth of myths, legends, fables, epics, proverbs, and folk tales, and each country's body of folk literature is tantalizingly similar to that found in other countries.

One theory holds that folk literature the world over is basically similar, not only because it was carried from one place to another, but also because people everywhere have always had the same needs and aspirations. They have been concerned with earning a living and providing a comfortable refuge for themselves away from harm and danger. They have struggled to earn love and acceptance from others, and they have worked to accomplish something worthy of respect. People have always searched diligently for knowledge and information. They have managed in various ways to bring an element of romance and beauty into their lives.

It is understandable that these basic tasks of life have been the source and subject of man's literature down through the ages and doubtless will continue to be so in the future. Several years ago, in her classic book on storytelling, Carolyn Bailey wrote about the significance of folklore on a society:

> The eternal soul of a nation is expressed in its folklore. It is remembered when all else is forgotten. A people may lose fame or even disappear from the face of the earth because of the cruelty of other nations, but its tales remain and are cherished. And they should be cherished by those who tell stories to children, for in them are the ingredients that make for a perfect story. They have all the elements of adventure, entertainment and education.[1]

Out of the abundant riches in folklore available to today's students, folk tales remain the favorite of young children. Because these old stories were handed down by word of mouth for so many years, they have become streamlined and stripped of all nonessential elements. Such stark simplicity makes them perfect for storytelling, and very appealing to children, who are always anxious to get to the heart of the matter.

One criterion for excellence in children's stories is that they should appeal to adults as well as children. Folk tales measure up. Their uncanny power to entertain and enchant people of all ages has caused them to survive thousands of years. "To believe in magic wands, gingerbread houses, talking scarecrows, glass slippers, wishing caps, elves, and trolls is to enter a make-believe world which spans both nations and generations."[2]

Although entertainment was the basic intent of the folk tales, a broader viewpoint would also acknowledge the high moral value and warm humanism to be found in them. The imagery created when a folktale is well told has the power to touch the deepest of human feelings and emotions. In a vicarious way it serves to allay fears, to fulfill ambitions, and to provide love. It strengthens, renews, and leaves the listener ready to resume the struggles and stresses of everyday living.

1. Carolyn S. Bailey, *The Story-Telling Hour* (New York: Dodd, Mead & Co., 1934), p. 49.
2. Carole Mosley Kirkton, "Once Upon a Time . . . Folk Tales and Storytelling," *Elementary English* 48 (1971): 1024.

According to Arbuthnot, the old folk tales are unsurpassed as a means of showing children the world the way it is and the way it ought to be:

> Stories such as "Cinderella," "Three Little Pigs," "Three Billy Goats Gruff," and "Snow White" dramatize the stormy conflict of good and evil. And they reiterate the old verities that kindness and goodness will triumph over evil if they are backed by wisdom, wit, and courage. These basic truths we should like built into the depths of the child's consciousness; they are the folk tales' great contribution to the child's social consciousness.[3]

The renowned poet and storyteller Padraic Colum also has great faith in the value of folk literature. He feels that the voice of a good storyteller has the ability to heighten the impact of a tale and make it remembered long after the telling: "The human voice, when it can really charge itself with what is in a poem or a story, more powerfully than any other agency, can put into our deeper consciousness those lasting patterns which belong to the deeper consciousness of the race.[4]

Marcia Brown, an author-illustrator who has won the Caldecott Award twice and was a runner-up six times, has turned again and again to folk literature for inspiration. She tells us that that the folktales are deeply true to life, and explains why they are needed by today's children:

> The heritage of childhood is the sense of life bequeathed to it by the folk wisdom of the ages . . . fairy tales are revelations of sober everyday fact. They are the abiding dreams and realities of the human soul.
>
> This very day some rogue has by his quick wit opened a new world to his master and helped him win the princess of his heart, to whom he is entitled by sensibilities if not by birth.
>
> Today a staunch soldier, through circumstances not of his own making, goes through terrible trials, but remains steadfast in his devotion to his ideal.
>
> Tonight somewhere Cinderella, through the magic of kindness, has been enchanted into greatest beauty; tonight Cinderella goes to her ball to meet her prince.[5]

More and more modern educators are beginning to view the systematic study of folk literature as a necessary component of the young child's curriculum. It is now believed that high school and college students can more

3. May Hill Arbuthnot, *Children and Books,* 4th ed. (Glenview, Ill.: Scott, Foresman and Co., 1972), p. 20.

4. Padraic Colum, *Story Telling New and Old* (New York: The Macmillan Co., 1968), p. 21.

5. Helen W. Painter, "Marcia Brown: A Study in Versatility," *Elementary English* 43 (1966): 855.

easily acquire an adequate understanding and appreciation of the great literature introduced at those levels if they have had the advantage of hearing folk tales in early childhood. Fortunately, this philosophy is bringing about a revival of interest in the heritage of poetry and story:

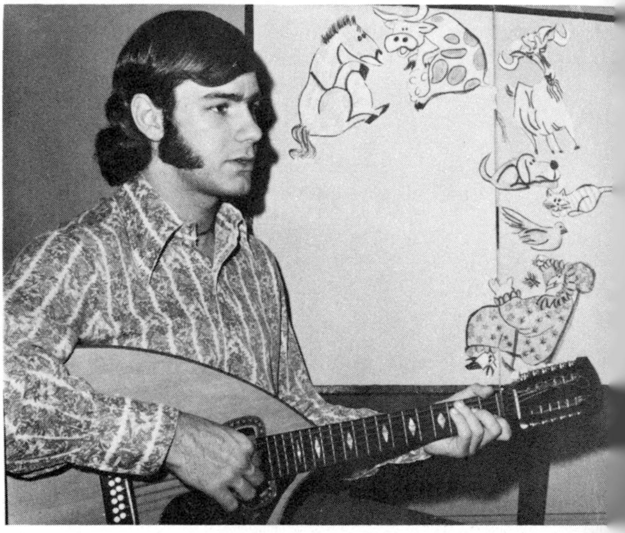

Fig. 2.1. Folklore and folk music have always been closely related, and the modern storyteller is often accompanied by the guitar, harp or ukulele. In this photograph, flannelboard cut-outs are used to illustrate the repetitive tale, "I Know an Old Lady Who Swallowed a Fly." (Courtesy of H. L. Coody.)

> For without some ability for making ourselves at home in the world of thought, imagination, intuition, a boy or a girl will never be able to understand all that is summed up in art and philosophy, will never have any deep feeling for religion, and will not be able to get anything out of the reading of history; in short, unless they are somewhat at home in that world, they will live without any fineness in their lives.[6]

Telling Folk Tales to Children

Even though early storytellers created their stories with adults in mind and told them mainly to audiences of men and women, we know that the children had a way of listening in. As has always been the case, they took from the adult stories those parts that held meaning and interest for them and simply ignored (or promptly forgot) the rest. When adults realize that even young children are equipped with the amazing ability to discard those things that are irrelevant, they will never again be guilty of "watering down" literature before presenting it to them. On the con-

6. Colum, op. cit., p. 22.

trary, oral interpretation of literature should lead children to greater depths of understanding:

> The storyteller must have respect for the child's mind and the child's conception of the world, knowing it for a complete mind and a complete conception. If a storyteller have that respect he need not be childish in his language in telling stories to children. If the action be clear and the sentences clear one can use a mature language. Strange words, out-of-the- way words do not bewilder children if there be order in the action and in the sentences.[7]

It may seem paradoxical to discuss the ancient art of storytelling as a modern teaching procedure, but, nevertheless, it would be difficult to find any teaching practice in the modern curriculum that is more effective or one that is more favored by children.

According to Dewey Chambers, the teacher who tells stories as a pedagogical technique is employing an educational procedure that has been used by some of the world's greatest teachers: "Jesus used it, as did Plato, Confucius, and other great philosophers and teachers. It is an instructional technique that did not belong only in the past. It has relevance to today's teacher, as well. The modern teacher who employs this technique as a teaching tool is using an ancient method that is as modern as tomorrow."[8]

In the past few years, both pre-service and in-service programs for teachers have emphasized the importance of storytelling as a means of elevating literature to its rightful place in the early childhood curriculum. However, many teachers have yet to be converted to the art of storytelling as a basic teaching procedure, and to folk literature as an open sesame to the world of reading.

The Storyteller

Once a commitment is made to the efficacy of storytelling, it is possible for any teacher, aide, librarian, parent, or other interested adult to become an effective teller of tales to young children.

Each potential storyteller has a lifetime of experiences from which to draw, and with practice can become quite skillful at using life's experiences to enrich and enliven stories. "So, making a good storyteller is like making a good forest or garden or home or person. It is a way of life, in which a channel is opened through which may pour all the background,

7. Colum, op. cit., p. 13.
8. Dewey W. Chambers, *Literature for Children: Storytelling and Creative Drama* (Dubuque, Iowa: Wm. C. Brown Co. Publishers, 1970), p. 43.

experiences, awareness, skill, artistry, which you can possess and can develop."[9]

Ruth Sawyer feels that the most successful storytellers are those who are able to enjoy nature, to see beauty in everyday experiences:

> To be a good storyteller one must be gloriously alive. It is not possible to kindle fresh fires from burned-out embers. I have noticed that the best of traditional storytellers whom I have heard have been those who live close to the heart of things—to the earth, the sea, wind and weather. They have been those who knew solitude, silence. They reach constantly for understanding. They have come to know the power of the spoken word.[10]

If the storytelling venture is to be of maximum worth to children, a great deal of time, energy, and effort are demanded of the teacher. Hours must be spent in studying children's literature, in seeking the right stories, in learning, preparing and practicing each story for telling, in setting the stage for storytelling, and in providing appropriate follow-up activities to the stories. An apathetic teacher will never be an effective storyteller.

Many of the great storytellers have felt compelled to warn the beginner that storytelling takes effort. Marie Shedlock writes:

> . . . I maintain that capacity for work, and even drudgery, is among the essentials of storytelling. Personally, I know of nothing more interesting than watching the story grow gradually from mere outline into a dramatic whole. It is the same pleasure, I imagine, which is felt over the gradual development of a beautiful design on a loom. I do not mean machine-made work, which has to be done under adverse conditions in a certain time and which is similar to thousands of other pieces of work; but that work upon which we can bestow unlimited time and concentrated thought.[11]

Selecting the Story

In choosing a story to tell in nursery school, kindergarten, or the primary grades, the teacher might keep in mind the following criteria to insure that time spent in selecting, preparing, and telling the story will be worth the effort expended:

1. Is the story interesting and entertaining to you, the storyteller?
2. Does the story fit your personality, style and talents?

9. Ruth Tooze, *Storytelling* (Englewood Cliffs, N. J.: Prentice-Hall, Inc., 1959), pp. 28-29.

10. Ruth Sawyer, *The Way of the Storyteller* (New York: The Viking Press, 1962), p. 29.

11. Marie L. Shedlock, *The Art of the Story-Teller* (New York: Dover Publications, Inc., 1951), p. 28.

3. Will the story appeal to the interests of the children for whom it is intended?
4. Is the story appropriate to the age and ability level of the children?
5. Is the story brief enough for young listeners, with a minimum of characters and events?
6. Is there ample dialogue and action in the story?
7. Are there few lengthy descriptive passages and can they be easily condensed?
8. Will the story be relatively easy to prepare?
9. Will the story add variety and contrast to the storyteller's repertoire of stories?
10. Is it a story that would be better told than read aloud?

Of course, these are not the only features to be considered in the selection of a story, but if the storyteller is able to give an affirmative answer to the questions listed, the story being considered has a much better chance of meeting the needs and interests of children than another story chosen at random.

There is no guarantee of success in storytelling. Careful planning and preparation can only reduce the risks. Storytelling is as highly personal as any of the other arts. A story may have instant appeal for one group and leave another completely unmoved. When a story does fail to captivate a group, the storyteller would be wise to analyze the situation and find out why. Constant evaluation and appraisal are necessary measures for perfecting the art of storytelling.

It would be impossible to enumerate the benefits that accrue to young children when a story is well chosen and well told. Some of the most obvious values of effective storytelling are:

1. It introduces the child to some of the finest literature available.
2. It acquaints the child with an array of cultures from around the world.
3. It brings to the child many characters with whom he can identify.
4. It creates a wholesome relationship between a child and an adult.
5. It helps the child to better understand life, to establish worthy goals and purposes for himself.
6. It whets the appetite for further literary experiences, and creates an interest in reading.
7. It enriches and enlarges the vocabulary.
8. It improves listening and comprehension skills.
9. It stimulates creative writing and other creative activities.
10. It provides the child with valuable information and knowledge.

Preparing the Story

To memorize a story for telling verbatim is usually a mistake. In the first place such a procedure is entirely too time consuming, and a dearth of stories would inevitably be the result for most teachers. Secondly, a memorized story lacks the warmth, naturalness, and spontaneity needed to give it life and breath. And finally, when a story has been memorized word for word, there is always the danger that forgotten lines may throw the storyteller off course and spoil the story completely.

A more practical and realistic plan is recommended by many experienced storytellers. It calls for memorizing only certain passages from a story and for learning the rest by scenes or "pictures" as they appear in the story. Since this plan has a great deal of merit for the novice storyteller, it will be more fully discussed on the following pages.

Because the opening or introduction to a story should be presented as close to perfect as possible if it is to capture the interest and imagination of children, memorization or near-memorization of this part is justifiable.

A typical folk tale's introduction is disarmingly brief and simple, and yet it usually presents the characters, the time, the place, and perhaps a hint of the conflict to be resolved. One of the favorite tales from the Grimm Brothers, "The Fisherman and His Wife," opens in this way:

> There was once a fisherman and his wife. They lived together in a vinegar jug close by the sea, and the fisherman went there every day and fished: and he fished and he fished.[12]

Characteristic of the old folk tales is a regularly recurring phrase or verse. As far as children are concerned, this repetition is one of the most appealing features in literature. The young listeners expect (and deserve) to hear a story's refrain repeated accurately each time, and for this reason it should also be memorized. Actually, it is the easiest part of a story to learn. The same rhythm that enchants children virtually sings its way into the storyteller's memory. Listen to the rhythm of the refrain in "The Fisherman and His Wife":

> Manye, Manye, Timpie Tee,
> Fishye, Fishye in the sea,
> Ilsebill my wilful wife
> Does not want my way of life.[13]

Many storytellers maintain that a well-told conclusion is so vital to the success of a story that it should also be committed to memory. Many

12. Jacob and Wilhelm Grimm, *Tales from Grimm,* translated and illustrated by Wanda Gág (New York: Coward-McCann, Inc., 1936), p. 149.
13. Ibid., p. 151.

an otherwise good story has been ruined because the storyteller strung out the conclusion or allowed it to taper off to nothing. A good ending to a folk tale comes immediately after the climax. It is brief, concise, emphatic, and conclusive. "Snip, Snap, Snout. This tale's told out."[14]

The following outline is an informal way of making notations about the scenes of a story.[15] Key clues can help in learning the story and also in reviewing it for retelling.

The Three Billy Goats Gruff

I. Introduction
"Once upon a time there were three billy goats who were to go up to the hillside to make themselves fat, and the name of all three was 'Gruff'."

II. Development
   A. Troll under the bridge
   B. Youngest goat's crossing
      1. Goats' refrain: "Trip, trop! trip, trop!"
      2. Troll's refrains: "Who's that tripping over my bridge?" "Now, I'm coming to gobble you up!"
   C. Second goat's crossing

III. Climax
   A. Third goat's crossing
   B. Destruction of troll

IV. Conclusion
   A. Goats reach the hillside
   "Snip, Snap, Snout.
   This tale's told out."

Once the scenes of a story are clearly in mind, the storyteller needs to practice telling it several times, paying special attention to the introduction, climax, conclusion, and rhythmic refrain. Oral rehearsals should be repeated until the story is completely mastered.

Creating a Climate

To give children a better opportunity for effective looking and listening, the teacher will wish to set the stage for storytelling. A low chair or

14. Marcia Brown, *The Three Billy Goats Gruff* (New York: Harcourt Brace Jovanovich, Inc., 1957).
15. Ibid.

stool for the storyteller is placed in the most advantageous spot in the classroom. It then becomes the focal point for the storytelling circle.

If aids or related objects are to be used with the story, a small desk or table to hold them may be placed beside the chair. All such items should be assembled and arranged, in the order they are to be presented, before the children are seated. Once the storyteller's station has been established and realia are in place, the children may then come to the area and seat themselves in a semicircle around the storyteller.

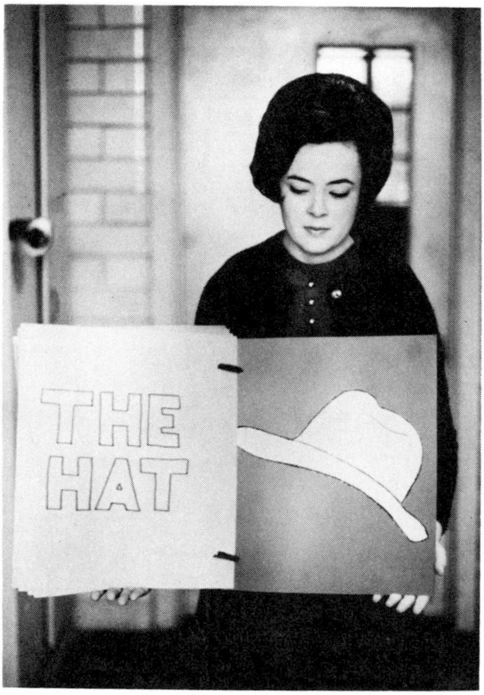

Fig. 2.2. To create an interest in the Newbery Award book, *Ginger Pye,* this primary teacher uses a flip chart to introduce the characters—telling just enough of their adventures to arouse curiosity. (Courtesy of Elizabeth Flynn.)

Various methods of providing seating for children in uncarpeted classrooms have proven successful. Some teachers prefer to have the children bring chairs to the circle. Others provide an area rug which is reserved solely for storytelling and reading aloud. Still other teachers have obtained inexpensive cushions on which the children can comfortably sit cross-legged. If cushions are used, they may be stored in a large box or basket that the children have decorated with bright poster paint. Alternatives to cushions might include carpet samples, bath towels, foam rubber squares, or mats made by stitching several thicknessses of cloth together.

Fortunately, more and more kindergarten and primary classrooms are being carpeted, and floor space is being utilized to give children some sorely needed leg room. Many newer classes are being designed and built with a "story well"—a sunken, carpeted circle lined with soft benches for snug, intimate seating. The story well is an updated version of the primitive "story ring" composed of logs and arranged around an open campfire.

Many seating arrangements are possible. A teacher may wish to experiment with more than one type. In any case, the seating of the children should add to the ceremonial ritual of the storytelling period. The established routine of preparing for a story in a special way offers young children a certain kind of security. It also conjures up the feeling that magic and excitement are just around the corner. Once the mood is created, the storyteller's task is one of pure delight.

Fig. 2.3. Every child in a storytelling group should be able to get close enough to see and hear and to take an active part in the experience. An area rug can be transformed into a magic carpet. (Courtesy of South Park Independent School District, Beaumont, Texas.)

Setting the Time

There is probably no "best" time of the day to tell stories in the classroom. Some teachers prefer to use storytelling at various intervals during the day to give children a break from tedious mental tasks. This is a sound plan, since there is evidence that they are able to take up their work again, rested, refreshed, and with a renewed interest that allows them to accomplish more.

Story time is used by other teachers as a way to calm children and settle them down when they arrive in the classroom. A "decompression chamber" is the way one teacher refers to the early morning story circle, a place where children are able to put aside some of the anxieties they bring with them to school.

Story time is used by many kindergarten teachers as a means of calling children from their work at interest centers when it is time for planning, for directed activities, or for evaluation. (One teacher claps two small wooden blocks together to summon children, just the way oriental storytellers have done for centuries.) For the most part, children do not like having to leave the interest centers, and storytelling serves to soften what could amount to an unhappy transition for many of them.

Fig. 2.4. Animal stories read or told to children remind them of their own experiences with pets and animals, and provide ideas for creative writing. (Courtesy of Saint Thomas Episcopal School, College Station, Texas.)

One plan that should be carefully considered by all teachers of young children is the practice of telling a story just before children leave for home. The satisfying experience of sharing a good story with other children and with the teacher is a nearly foolproof way to insure that each child leaves with a positive feeling about school. Such an attitude is reflected to parents when the child relates the activities of the school day. Thus, storytelling becomes a way of improving home-school relations in which the child becomes the beneficiary in the long run.

Barriers to Good Storytelling

Certain limitations and problems exist in the practice of telling stories to young children. Fortunately, they are difficulties that can be predicted, anticipated, and subsequently resolved. Many master storytellers have issued warnings to those who are novices in the art, with the hope that their years of trial and error experiences could be of assistance to the beginner. Some of their most helpful suggestions are as follows:

1. The storyteller should avoid using moralizing stories with strong didactic overtones. Such stories only serve to offend the sensibilities of children and leave them with a feeling of having been "preached to" by one who lured them into the situation on the promise of entertainment.
2. Over-acting, making too many gestures, and talking down to children are flaws that can cause a story to fall short or fail completely. Storytellers should remain true to their art and refuse to engage in practices that turn it into a tortured performance. Children can see that kind of production any hour of the day on television. Storytelling is, and must remain, an experience of higher quality.
3. There should be no attempt to analyze every story told. Interested children will ask questions, and discussions should take place in a natural way. The storyteller may wish to ask leading, provocative questions, which is quite acceptable, but this part of the storytelling session should be informal and spontaneous. Ultimately, each child should have the freedom of interpreting the literature in his own way.
4. Listeners should not be *required* to retell a story or to react to it in other ways. Children frequently choose to write about a story they have enjoyed, to interpret it in painting, or to act it out. Of course, this privilege should always be extended, but experiences with literature are too personal and individualized to demand the same kind of feedback from all the children in a group.
5. Distracting influences should not be consistently tolerated by the storyteller. If a story is worth telling, it deserves a respectful, interested, attentive audience. Many stories have been spoiled for all the listeners because a few children were allowed to wander

in and out of the listening group, to play with distracting objects, or to make irrelevant, extraneous comments. Effective listening can be taught and storytelling is a reliable means of doing it.

Using Visual Aids

Purists in the field of storytelling often criticize the use of aids to enhance a story and view them only as distracting elements. On the other hand, teachers who make a practice of telling stories frequently to the same children over the span of a school year recognize the need for variety in the routine of storytelling.

In most cases, teachers of older elementary students rely solely on the story itself and the human voice to carry it forward, while teachers of younger children make frequent use of the flannelboard, pocket chart, flip chart, pictures, records, puppets, cut-outs, and related objects to illustrate and dramatize a story. Paul Anderson defends the use of graphic devices to hold the attention of young children:

> When Hans Christian Anderson entertained the children of Denmark with his stories, he used to cut out silhouettes in order to make his characters more vivid. In ancient China the storyteller would cast shadows to illustrate the characters in his tales of magic and ancient ways. The modern movie cartoon favorites use a combination of silhouette figures and movement to hold attention. In the modern classroom, the flannelboard provides the storyteller with the means of achieving similar types of movement, magic and characterization.[16]

It would seem plausible that, by using aids as a motivating introduction to a story or as a graphic follow-up activity to a story, the two viewpoints could be reconciled. Visual aids could serve their purpose of making the story more interesting and understandable, while the story itself could be presented completely unadorned and true to the ancient style of storytelling.

Once the flannelboard or pocket chart has been used to illustrate a story, it should be left in place for a few days as an interest center for the children. A great deal of oral language is stimulated as children manipulate the cut-outs, and tell their own version of the story.

Paper and pellon cut-outs for the flannelboard or pocket chart may be conveniently stored in file folders labeled with the title of the story.[17] If the cue card or outline used in learning the story is filed along with the

16. Paul S. Anderson, *Language Skills in Elementary Education* (New York: The Macmillan Co., 1964), p. 299.
17. Pellon is a fabric used in sewing to stiffen collars and cuffs.

Fig. 2.5. This "involvement" bulletin board was prepared cooperatively by second grade students and their teacher. It was an outgrowth of a storytelling session in which the children had become acquainted with Katy-No-Pockets and her baby.

visuals, it becomes a simple matter for the teacher or aide to retrieve and review the story for presentation at a later date. Fortunately for the storyteller, children request the same stories over and over again.

By adding a few stories each year to a story file, a teacher is able to accumulate a good supply. On hand will be stories for telling on all holidays and special occasions, along with many other stories to make a routine school day not so routine.

The following story invites listener participation. Each time the storyteller pauses, the children should join in and repeat the refrain, "Cheese, peas, and chocolate pudding."[18]

CHEESE, PEAS, AND CHOCOLATE PUDDING

There was once a little boy who ate cheese, peas, and chocolate pudding. Cheese, peas, and chocolate pudding. Cheese, peas, and chocolate pudding. Every day the same old thing: cheese, peas, and chocolate pudding.

18. Betty Van Witsen, "Cheese, Peas, and Chocolate Pudding," *Believe and Make-Believe,* edited by Lucy Sprague Mitchell and Irma Simonton Black. (New York: Bank Street College of Education, 1956) pp. 31-34. Copyright © 1956 by Bank Street College of Education. Used with permission of the College.

For breakfast, he would have some cheese. Any kind. Cream cheese, American cheese, Swiss cheese, Dutch cheese, Italian cheese, blue cheese, green cheese, yellow cheese, brick cheese. Even Liederkrantz. Just cheese for breakfast.

For lunch he ate peas. Green peas or yellow peas. Frozen peas, canned peas, dried peas, split peas, black-eyed peas. No potatoes, though; just peas for lunch.

And for supper he would have cheese *and* peas. And chocolate pudding. Cheese, peas, and chocolate pudding. Cheese, peas, and chocolate pudding. Every day the same old thing: cheese, peas, and chocolate pudding.

Once his mother bought a lamb chop for him. She cooked it in a little frying pan on the stove, and she put some salt on it, and gave it to the little boy on a blue dish. The boy looked at it. He smelled it (it did smell delicious!). He even touched it. But—

"Is this cheese?" he asked.

"It's a lamb chop, darling," said his mother. The boy shook his head.

"Cheese!" he said. So his mother ate the lamb chop herself, and the boy had some cottage cheese.

One day his big brother was chewing a raw carrot. It sounded so good, the little boy reached his hand out for a bite.

"Sure!" said his brother, "Here!" The little boy *almost* put the carrot into his mouth, but at the last minute he remembered, and said, "Is this peas?"

"No, it's a carrot," said his brother.

"Peas," said the little boy firmly, handing the carrot back.

Once his daddy was eating a big dish of raspberry pudding. It looked so shiny red and cool, the little boy came over and held his mouth open.

"Want a taste?" asked his daddy. The little boy looked and looked at the raspberry pudding. He almost looked it off the dish.

"But, is it chocolate pudding?" he asked.

"No, it's raspberry pudding," said Daddy. So the little boy frowned and backed away.

"Chocolate pudding!" he said.

His grandma bought him an ice cream cone. The little boy just shook his head.

His aunt and uncle invited him for a fried chicken dinner. Everybody ate fried chicken and fried chicken and more fried chicken. Except the little boy. And you know what he ate.

Cheese, peas, and chocolate pudding. Cheese, peas and chocolate pudding. Every day the same old thing: cheese, peas, and chocolate pudding.

But one day—ah, one day a very funny thing happened. The little boy was playing puppy. He lay on the floor and growled and barked and rolled over. He crept to the table where his big brother was having lunch.

"Arf-arf!" he barked.

"Good doggie!" said his brother, patting his head. The little boy lay down on his back on the floor, and barked again.

But at that minute, his big brother dropped a piece of *something*.

Something dropped into the little boy's mouth. He sat up in surprise. Because *something* was on his tongue. And *something* was warm and juicy and delicious!

And it didn't taste like cheese. And it did *not* taste like peas. And it certainly wasn't chocolate pudding.

The little boy chewed slowly. Each chew tasted better. He swallowed *something*.

"That's not cheese," he said.

"No, it's not," said his brother.

"And it isn't peas."

"No, not peas," said his brother.

"It couldn't be chocolate pudding."

"No, it certainly is not chocolate pudding," smiled his brother. "It's hamburger."

The little boy thought hard. "I like hamburger," he said.

So ever after that, the little boy ate cheese, peas, chocolate pudding, and hamburger.

Until he was your age, of course. When he was your age, he ate everything.

The following is a popular story that lends itself to flannelboard presentation. It may be used at various seasons by showing the head as made of a jack-o-lantern, a valentine, a shamrock, or an Easter egg. The children think a teacher is very ingenious to be able to make their favorite story fit the season at hand.[19]

QUEER COMPANY

A little old woman lived all alone in a little old house in the woods. One Halloween she sat in the corner, and as she sat, she spun.

Still she sat and
Still she spun and
Still she wished for company.

19. Paul S. Anderson, "Queer Company," *Flannelboard Stories for the Primary Grades* (Minneapolis, Minn.: T. S. Denison & Co., Inc., 1962) pp. 30-31. Copyright © 1962 by T. S. Denison & Co., Inc. Reprinted by permission of the publisher.

Then she saw her door open a little way, and in came
A pair of big, big feet
And sat down by the fireside.
"That is very strange," thought the little old woman, but—
Still she sat and
Still she spun and
Still she wished for company.
Then in came
A pair of small, small legs,
And sat down on the big, big feet.
"Now that is very strange." thought the old woman, but—
Still she sat and
Still she spun and
Still she wished for company.
Then in came
A wee, wee waist,
And sat right down on the small, small legs.
"Now that is very strange," thought the old woman, but—
Still she sat and
Still she spun and
Still she wished for company.
Then in came
A pair of broad, broad shoulders,
And sat down on the wee, wee waist.
But—
Still she sat and
Still she spun and
Still she wished for company.
Then in through the door came
A pair of long, long arms,
And sat down on the broad, broad shoulders.
"Now that is very strange," thought the little old woman, but—
Still she sat and
Still she spun and
Still she wished for company.
Then in came
A pair of fat, fat hands,
And sat down on the long, long arms.
But—
Still she sat and
Still she spun and
Still she wished for company.

Then in came
A round, round head,
And sat down on top of all
That sat by the fireside.
The little old woman stopped her spinning and asked
"Where did you get such big feet?"
"By much tramping, by much tramping," said Somebody.
"Where did you get such small, small legs?"
"By much running, by much running," said Somebody.
"Where did you get such a wee, wee waist?"
"Nobody knows, nobody knows," said Somebody.
"Where did you get such broad, broad shoulders?"
"From carrying brooms," said Somebody.
"Where did you get such long, long arms?"
"Swinging the scythe, swinging the scythe," said Somebody.
"Where did you get such fat, fat hands?"
"By working, by working," said Somebody.
"How did you get a huge, huge head?"
"Of a pumpkin I made it," said Somebody.
"Then said the little old woman,
"What did you come for?"
"YOU!" said Somebody.

The ancient art of storytelling remains as effective today as it ever was. It is an art form that can easily compete with television, movies, and recordings. In the midst of visual and auditory bombardment vying for his attention, the child wants and needs to hear stories told by a storyteller who commands a quiet confidence.

Teachers of young children have a responsibility for sharing with them the great stories of the past, but they also should show them how modern writers are creating tales that mirror our culture, tales that will eventually take their place alongside the classics. This generation is producing its own hero stories, legends, myths, and proverbs—folklore that will find its way into the mainstream of literature, to be read and told, pondered over and wondered about in ages to come.

CHILDREN'S BOOKS FOR STORYTELLING

Favorite Stories for the Children's Hour, edited by Carolyn Sherwin Bailey and Clara M. Lewis. New York: Platt & Munk, Publishers, 1965. An anthology of favorite folk tales, fables, and legends. The collection is made up of some of the most popular stories from the hundreds written and retold by Carolyn Bailey.

The Man in the Moon, written by Alta Jablow and Carl Withers and illustrated by Peggy Wilson. New York: Holt, Rinehart & Winston, Inc., 1969. A pair of noted anthropologists and folklorists collaborated on this collection of tales about the sun, moon, and stars—celestial stories from all parts of the world.

Merry Tales for Children, by Carolyn Sherwin Bailey. New York: Platt & Munk, Publishers, 1943. A series of humorous short stories to be read and told to young children. The stories are divided into subject categories: home stories, animal stories, folk tales, and holiday stories.

More Tales from Grimm, translated and illustrated by Wanda Gág. New York: Coward-McCann, Inc., 1947. Wanda Gág died during the translation of this group of stories and the work was completed by her husband and sister. Fortunately, she had made at least one illustration for each of the stories, and this book is comparable in excellence to her others.

Stories for Little Children, by Pearl S. Buck. New York: The John Day Co., Inc., 1940. These short stories are episodes in the lives of five young children as they strive to understand such phenomena as daylight, darkness, and the seasons of the year.

Stories to Tell Boys and Girls, compiled and edited by Al Bryant. Grand Rapids, Mich.: Zonderman Publishing House, 1952. These stories were collected and arranged for the purpose of satisfying spiritual and moral needs of children. Each story is intended to teach a realistic lesson from life.

The Sun is a Golden Earring, written by Natalia M. Belting and illustrated by Bernarda Bryon. New York: Holt, Rinehart & Winston, Inc., 1962. Ancient legends from all parts of the world explaining how the sun, moon, stars, lightening, thunder, clouds, and winds came to be.

Tales from Grimm, translated and illustrated by Wanda Gág. Eau Claire, Wis.: E. M. Hale and Co., 1936. Wanda Gág made small black and white sketches to illustrate the tales as she translated them from the German. She is considered a perfect interpreter of Grimm in both text and pictures.

Tales of Grimm and Anderson, selected by Frederick Jacobi, Jr. New York: The Modern Library, 1952. The timeless tales of Anderson and the Grimms are combined in one volume. The introduction by W. H. Auden builds a case for using folk tales and fairy stories in the education of children.

Three Gay Tales from Grimm, translated and illustrated by Wanda Gág. New York: Coward-McCann, Inc., 1943. Three humorous "noodle" stories about foolish people who prosper in spite of their foolishness. The stories are "The Clever Wife," "The Three Fathers," and "Goose Hans."

Treasured Tales, compiled by Laura E. Mathon and Thusnelda Schmidt. New York: Abingdon Press, 1960. Great stories of courage, faith and bravery that have been told down through the ages. Hero stories retold by such writers as Eleanor Farjeon, Elizabeth Coatsworth, Kate Seredy, Maud Lindsay, and James Baldwin.

The World's Great Stories: 55 Legends that Live Forever, written by Louis Untermeyer and illustrated by Mae Gerhard. Philadelphia, Pa.: J. B. Lippincott, Co., 1964. "The Trojan Horse," "Daedalus and Icarus," "Romulus and Remus," and other stories loved by children have been rewritten by Louis Untermeyer to update the language and images for modern readers.

BIBLIOGRAPHY

Anderson, Paul S. *Flannelboard Stories for the Primary Grades.* Minneapolis, Minn.: T. S. Denison & Co., Inc., 1962.

———. *Language Skills in Elementary Education.* New York: The Macmillan Co., 1964.

Arbuthnot, May Hill. *Children and Books.* 3rd ed. Glenview, Ill.: Scott, Foresman and Co., 1964.

Bailey, Carolyn S. *The Story-Telling Hour.* New York: Dodd, Mead & Co., 1934.

Brown, Marcia. *The Three Billy Goats Gruff.* New York: Harcourt Brace Jovanovich, Inc., 1957.

Cameron, Eleanor. *The Green and Burning Tree.* Boston: Little, Brown & Co., 1969.

Chambers, Dewey W. *Literature for Children: Storytelling and Creative Drama.* Dubuque, Iowa: Wm. C. Brown Co. Publishers, 1970.

Colum, Padraic. *Story Telling New and Old.* New York: The Macmillan Co., 1968.

Grimm, Jacob, and Grimm, Wilhelm. Translated and illustrated by Wanda Gág. New York: Coward-McCann, Inc., 1936.

Kirkton, Carole Mosley. "Once Upon a Time . . . Folk Tales and Storytelling." *Elementary English* 48 (1971):1024.

Mitchell, Lucy Sprague, and Black, Irma Simonton, eds. *Believe and Make-Believe.* New York: Bank Street College of Education, 1956.

Moore, Vardine. *Pre-School Hour.* New York: The Scarcecrow Press, Inc., 1966.

Painter, Helen W. "Marcia Brown: A Study in Versatility." *Elementary English* 43 (1966):855.

Sawyer, Ruth. *The Way of the Storyteller.* New York: The Viking Press, 1962.

Shedlock, Marie L. *The Art of the Story-Teller.* New York: Dover Publications, Inc., 1951.

Tooze, Ruth. *Storytelling.* Englewood Cliffs, N. J.: Prentice-Hall, Inc., 1959.

3

"Let's Act It Out": Literature for Dramatization

The use of dramatization as an educational procedure is unsurpassed as a means of helping children interpret and understand literature. Such dramatization might be defined as play-making jointly planned and executed by the children and their teacher. No written script is involved; no lines are memorized. Few, if any, properties or costumes are required. In spite of this lack of structure, or perhaps because of it, young children take their roles quite seriously. They imitate characters and act out scenes with a freedom of imagination to rival the greatest of professional actors.

Scholars in the fields of anthropology and psychology tell us that imitation is primal in man. Paintings, sculpture, music, dance, drama, and literature handed down to us from the past all testify that man has long had within him an innate urge to imitate. He not only has imitated other men, but animals, plants, and natural phenomena. Through such imitation he has attempted to understand others. Above all, he has sought to understand himself and his own purpose in life.

Most teachers recognize that young children need to act out their fantasies in wholesome ways, and thus many opportunities are provided for them to do so. Rudolph and Cohen explain the importance of fantasizing in which children are able to imitate or act out what (at least for the moment) they would like to be:

> The world of make-believe has an almost real quality for children and they can pretend within a wide range of possible behavior. They can wish themselves anything they like, and play that it becomes a reality. They can pretend to be glib and powerful and authoritative, even if they really are only little children with very little power indeed. They can pretend that they are angry tigers, growling dogs, and fierce lions, even if in reality they are gentle and well-mannered boys and girls. They can try on for size the feeling of being a mother, a father, a street cleaner, or a truck driver. They can go back to babyhood or forward to adulthood, they can frighten others or be the thing they are themselves afraid of. This inner life of children we call their fantasy life and it represents an integral part of children's efforts to comprehend themselves and the world around them.[1]

Informal creative drama usually begins with a literature experience. No matter whether the teacher chooses to read aloud one of the popular contemporary stories, tell a favorite old folk tale, recite an appealing poem, or sing a Mother Goose rhyme, the children involved should be afforded an opportunity to give personal expression to the literature. Dramatization is the most natural and child-like means of expression.

Because there is no better way to make literature come alive for children, a well-balanced literature program should include all forms of dramatization that are suitable for young children—dramatic play, pantomime, creative dramatics, and puppetry.

Dramatic Play

Dramatic play is the acting out of life roles and situations. It is unstructured, and for the most part, unsupervised. Ordinarily, there is no costumery, no prescribed dialogue, and no audience. A child simply "plays like" he is a father, a policeman, a bear, a horse, or perhaps a character from literature.

Although dramatic play is frequently enjoyed by children at all levels in the primary grades, it probably reaches its peak in nursery school and kindergarten. Interest centers (sometimes called learning centers, and more recently, "involvement" centers) are used at those levels, mainly for the purpose of enriching the quality of dramatic play. Tantalizing

1. Marguerita Rudolph and Dorothy H. Cohen, *Kindergarten, A Year of Learning* (New York: Appleton-Century-Crofts, 1964), p. 58.

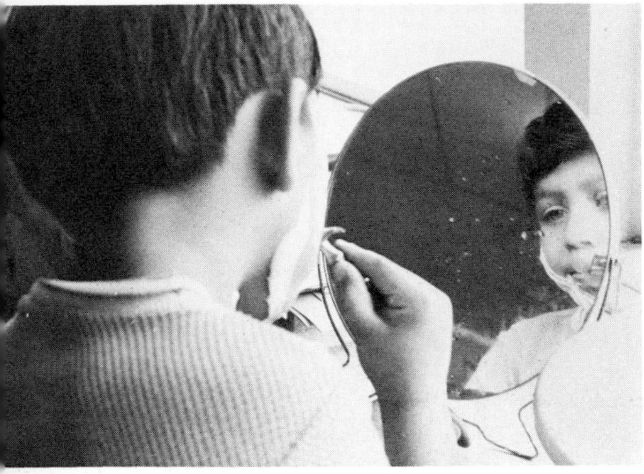

Fig. 3.1. Very few properties are needed in dramatic play. The main ingredient is the child's own imagination. (Courtesy of South Park Independent School District, Beaumont, Texas.)

materials and equipment are arranged for easy accessibility in separate areas around the classroom. Child-sized tables are filled with objects that encourage curiosity, manipulation, and "play like."

Some teachers provide a small store front that can be easily converted into a grocery store, post office, bank, shoe store, hamburger stand, ice cream parlor, beauty or barber shop, flower shop, drugstore, or any other establishment the children happen to be interested in at the moment. To accompany the various occupations and professions inspired by the store front, a series of "prop" boxes may be supplied. A box might contain, for example, a nurse's cap, a stethoscope, and a hot water bottle, or a chef's hat, an apron, and a pancake turner. Only a few properties are needed. The main ingredient will be the child's imagination. It is generally agreed, however, that children learn more from dramatic play when a trained, interested adult knows how to spark and nourish it.

A careful observation of children at work in interest centers will quickly reveal the fact that they re-create and re-enact past experiences

Fig. 3.2. Dramatic play is the spontaneous acting out of life's roles, and interest centers enrich the quality of dramatic play. (Courtesy of South Park Independent School District, Beaumont, Texas.)

through play. Their past experiences include meaningful encounters with literature. In the housekeeping center children may be acting out the adventures of Papa Small, Mama Small, and the Small Smalls. In the building block area, other children may be working on a snug harbor for Little Toot or an airport for Loopy. A new chair for Peter and another for Baby Bear may be under construction in the woodworking corner. This kind of healthy fantasizing about characters goes on day after day wherever and whenever it is allowed to flourish. Thus it is that dramatic play and literature are inextricably bound together, and both are an integral part of the early childhood curriculum.

Pantomime

Pantomime is the ancient art of telling a story with bodily movements only—without benefit of dialogue. Records show that it was present in primitive societies, expressing itself in war dances, animal mimicry rites, and in rituals of sacrifice. Later, it became popular to act out the lives of saints in mime fashion; eventually masks, properties and music were added to pantomime as an art form.

Pantomime has a place in today's classroom as an excellent means of studying literature. Children learn to understand and appreciate literature as they silently interpret it in pantomime form, while other children gain similar understandings by watching the performance.

Many children have had little or no experience with pantomime, but the teacher need only to illustrate the procedure by acting out, in mime fashion, a familiar piece of action or characterization from literature. Robert Whitehead writes about children's interest in mimesis and the teacher's part in encouraging it:

> Children find pantomime activities to be genuine fun, and literature comes alive as children give lifelike reenactments of situations and characters from books and stories. This is especially true if the teacher is willing to demonstrate techniques through her own pantomimes, and if she shows sincerity and empathy with the children in their interpretations of characters and scenes.[2]

Children may choose to pantomime only one scene from a story or poem, or they may wish to re-enact an entire piece of literature as the teacher reads it aloud part by part. It should be kept in mind that pantomime is based solely on movement. Each gesture or motion should be

2. Robert Whitehead, *Children's Literature: Strategies of Teaching* (Englewood Cliffs, N. J.: Prentice-Hall, Inc., 1968), p. 169.

clear-cut, purposeful, distinct, and realistic, in order that the audience will have no difficulty in determining the character and the specific action. For this reason, stories and poems selected for pantomime should be thoroughly familiar to the audience. The effort it takes to make wise literary selections and to promote effective pantomime skills will pay dividends as children begin to show a keener interest in literature.

Creative Dramatics

Even though creative dramatics is informal, with no printed script or memorized lines, it is still more formal and structured than dramatic play. It is the making of a play, usually based on literature, by a group of children working under the guidance of a teacher or an aide. The play is designed to be presented before an audience of peers.

In creative dramatics, the dialogue is extemporaneous, but the children decide in advance which scenes will be re-enacted. They assign parts, prepare simple properties and costumes, and finally present the play, all in a brief period of time. Again, Robert Whitehead has done an excellent job of delineating the teacher's role during this period of high creative endeavor on the part of children :

> Through all of this the teacher serves in a supportive role, helping the children to visualize the scenes and characters, serving as a source of properties, and helping with room arrangement and staging. Once the play is in progress, the teacher melts into the background, coming forward only if the continuity of the play falters, or acting as a prompter if a bit of dialogue is momentarily displaced. When the informal dramatization is over, the teacher leads the class in an analysis of the production.[3]

Guidance on the teacher's part is needed to help children see that not every detail of a story need be dramatized. Some time must be spent in helping them to isolate the main events, to arrange them in sequential order, and to prepare them for dramatization. All this must be done in such a way that the plot and theme of the story remain identifiable to a youthful audience. Many children, both performers and viewers, have been disappointed with the results of a dramatization simply because not enough supportive assistance was given by the teacher during the early stages of planning the production.

If the literature is to pave the way for dramatization, it should be recognized that some books have more theatrical potential than others.

3. Ibid., p. 178.

Any dramatization experience will be more successful if the literature contains lively action and strong characterization. The following is a brief list of popular contemporary books that lend themselves well to creative dramatics:

Drummer Hoff by Barbara Emberley
The Happy Lion by Louise Fatio
Anatole and the Cat by Eve Titus
The Bears on Hemlock Mountain by Alice Dalgliesh
Finders Keepers by Will and Nicolas
Jeanne-Marie Counts Her Sheep by Françoise
Little Tim and the Brave Sea Captain by Edward Ardizzone
Mr. Penny by Marie Hall Ets
Play With Me by Marie Hall Ets
Seven Diving Ducks by Margaret Friskey
Henry-Fisherman by Marcia Brown
May I Bring a Friend? by Beatrice Schenk de Reginers

Puppetry

No one knows for sure where or when the art of puppetry originated, but it is known that the little actors were popular long before the time of Christ. Ancient tombs and burial grounds in all parts of the world have revealed carved figures, jointed in various ways to permit movement by hand.

The word "puppet" means "doll," but a puppet is actually much more than a doll. It is a man-made figure, moved by human effort for the purpose of entertaining or teaching an audience. A puppet is an extension of the human being who operates it. Bil Baird, one of the world's most famous puppeteers, describes the relationship between a puppet and its creator:

> . . . He is the result of the concept, the animation, and the design of some of us fallible creatures. We make either good puppets or bad ones, and although the puppets do succeed to some extent in filtering out the egos of their creators, some of our foibles seem to come through.[4]

Even though the term "puppet" refers to a doll, Marjorie Batchelder denies that it is a doll and warns teachers against calling it such. She believes that men and boys tend to reject puppets when they are mistakenly associated with dolls. In her classic handbook on puppetry, she writes:

> If your puppet looks like a doll, do something about it—loosen its joints, exaggerate its features, give it movement. Particularly among

4. Bil Baird, *The Art of the Puppet* (New York: The Macmillan Co., 1965), p. 223.

men, you will find a certain embarrassment about puppets, and it is because they are so often associated with dolls.[5]

Professional puppeteers look on their puppets not as dolls, but as mechanical actors operated by human endeavor. They consider the most important feature of any puppet to be its "humanized" movement. Shari Lewis, the popular puppeteer of television fame, discusses the loss of human quality in those puppets operated electronically by remote control:

Fig. 3.3. A kindergarten teacher in costume becomes a live puppet, and steps from the pages of *Raggedy Ann* to teach her students a lesson on book care. (Courtesy of Sue Miles.)

> . . . They are astounding and quite lifelike, but in my opinion, lack the spontaneity, charm, warmth, and humanity that can be found only when the puppeteer is in direct contact with his alter ego.[6]

A puppet may represent a person, an animal, a machine, or an abstraction, but no matter what form it takes, the art of puppetry is an ancient and effective way in which man expresses himself and communicates with others. Before the advent of television, it was a popular form of home entertainment. Fortunately, in homes where television has not been allowed to assume so important a role, children and their parents still have time for such activities as storytelling, reading aloud, and puppetry.

5. Marjorie Batchelder, *The Puppet Theatre Handbook* (New York: Harper & Row, Publishers, 1947), p. 15.
6. Shari Lewis, *Making Easy Puppets* (New York: E. P. Dutton & Co., Inc., 1967), p. 13.

By the same token, in classrooms that have not become over-mechanized, puppetry is still used to dramatize events in history, to illustrate ways of life in other cultures, to encourage acceptable social behavior, to emphasize desirable health practices, to stimulate creative activities, to promote literature, and simply to entertain children.

Puppetry is widely used as an educational practice during early childhood because teachers recognize the value of a puppet to help young children with personal development. It is nothing short of miraculous the way some children are able to express thoughts, ideas, and feelings through the mouth of a puppet with a fluency they could never achieve otherwise. Edward Mattil is one who sees the puppet as having therapeutic value for children who need to gain confidence in themselves:

> . . . There is probably no greater thrill or sense of satisfaction than that which comes to the teacher, who through planning and effort, finds his pupils unfolding and revealing qualities that had lain dormant. Often these very qualities are not evident because the child lacks confidence in himself or is unable to communicate his thoughts and feelings for lack of the right medium.[7]

Teachers who use puppets on a regular basis, just as they do other curriculum materials, vouch for their effectiveness as a means of developing self-confidence in shy children. Through the voice and gestures of the puppet, a child is able to say what he would like to say in real life situations, but does not in fear of disapproval or outright reprisal.

Through puppetry, the child controls his puppet, and in so doing, controls his environment. He can be as superior to his puppet as he wishes to be. It will do exactly as he commands. In this way a child is able to express hidden or suppressed emotions to a non-punishing audience. Release of this type is very important to healthy personality development.

Mattil makes an interesting statement regarding the benefits of classroom puppetry on the development of children. He sees puppets as a way to offset the limitations of the fragmented curriculum that is evident today in so many classrooms:

> In addition to the satisfaction of making a puppet, the child should have the opportunity to project even more of himself in the experience through performing. It is in this phase that children are able to express freely and openly some of the things which are difficult to express in the classroom. This is not to suggest that puppets are a catharsis; instead, they become a tool for easier and more open expression. The range of ideas and emotions are almost limitless in a puppet play

7. Edward L. Mattil, *Meaning in Crafts* (Englewood Cliffs, N. J.: Prentice-Hall, Inc., 1971), p. 91.

in which children are encouraged to give full play to their imaginations and their fantasies. The play or show culminates the activity, thus eliminating the fragmented or partial experience, so commonplace in education.[8]

Puppetry and Children's Literature

A young child seems to have an instinctive urge to imitate what he sees and hears. Acting out a concept is a child's way of demonstrating to himself and others that he understands. A good story told or read often needs to be imitated or acted out, and puppetry is a natural vehicle for this kind of drama.

Stories that can be readily adapted to puppet plays for and by young children are quite plentiful. The old folk tales with their humanism, their lively plots and realistic themes, are undoubtedly the best sources of material for puppetry. Economy of events and characters in the tales make puppet construction and staging relatively simple. The repetition and rhythmic language offer added appeal. Imagine Henny Penny, Cocky Locky and Ducky Lucky moving across the stage as stick puppets, shouting to all, "The sky is falling! The sky is falling! I must go and tell the king!"

In selecting stories to tell and read aloud, the teacher should keep in mind that children like lively dialogue, much action, a conflict to be resolved, heroes that *do* things, a rousing climax, and a satisfactory ending. Of course, these qualities are distinguishing characteristics of folk tales, and thus set them apart as ideal for puppet dramatization. The following list suggests some of the stories considered best for puppetry at the kindergarten and primary levels:

"The Three Little Pigs"
"The Three Billy Goats Gruff"
"The Three Bears"
"The Three Little Kittens"
"Jack and the Beanstalk"
"Henny Penny"
"The Pancake"
"The Little Red Hen and the Grain of Wheat"
"Bremen Town Musicians"
"Mr. and Mrs. Vinegar"
"Little Red Riding Hood"
"Cinderella"

8. Ibid., p. 103.

"Rumpelstiltskin"
"The Old Woman and Her Pig"
"Hansel and Gretel"
"The Wolf and the Seven Little Kids"

Puppet Types

Once the children have chosen a favorite tale to be dramatized, the next step is to decide which type of puppet will best represent the story characters. It is imperative that the teacher and the aide know many puppet types and how to make them. Materials for constructing various kinds of puppets should be easily accessible in order that children can make the puppets and hold an impromptu performance while interest in the story is at its peak.

Realism can be ignored in the art of puppet making. Exaggeration, imagination, and whimsy always make for better puppetry than does any attempt to duplicate nature. When children are provided with many interesting materials, and freedom to use them in fresh and original ways, they have the ability to create puppets that will bring pleasure both to themselves and to their audience.

An endless variety of puppets may be constructed from the four classic puppet types:

1. The hand puppet. This type, as the name implies, is made to fit over the hand of the puppeteer. The head of the puppet is usually moved by the puppeteer's index finger, and the arms are moved by his third finger and thumb. Some of the hand puppets are the easiest of all types to construct and manipulate.
2. The rod puppet. This type of puppet is controlled by one or more rigid rods to which the puppet is attached. In staging, the rod is usually hidden from view, and the puppet appears to move through space unassisted. Rod puppets are easily adaptable for use with children of all ages.
3. The shadow puppet. This type of puppet has been extremely popular in almost every culture. Early shadow puppets were made from the hides of animals. Figures were cut from the hide and fastened to a thin wire. When the figure was moved about between a bright light and a tightly stretched screen, a shadow or silhouette was seen by the audience. Modern children are able to produce very effective shadow puppet shows by means of the overhead projector and figures cut from black paper.
4. The marionette. This basic type of puppet is a jointed figure whose parts are manipulated by strings. Marionettes are the most difficult puppets to construct and to operate of all the puppet types. For the most

part marionettes are too intricate for young children to manage, even though they enjoy watching marionette performances staged by adults or older students. Because marionettes are better left to upper-grade students, they will not be given further consideration in this discussion of puppetry for young children. Directions for making a variety of puppets from the other three classic types are given on the following pages.

Puppet Construction

Paper Sack Puppets. A paper sack puppet is made by painting the face of a person or an animal on the folded end of a closed paper bag. The mouth of the face should be divided with the upper lip on the bottom of the paper bag and the lower lip on the bag itself. When the hand is placed inside the bag with fingers inside the flap, the puppet will open and close its mouth as the hand is opened and closed. Hair, ears, clothing, and other features may be made by gluing on bits of cloth, colored construction paper, costume jewelry, artificial flowers, or buttons and braid.

A puppet stage may consist of a chair or sofa, a table turned on its side, a doorway draped with a sheet, a chart rack, or a large cardboard carton.

Rubber Ball Puppets. The head of this type of puppet is made by cutting a hole inside a hollow rubber ball large enough for the puppeteer's index finger. Facial features are added to the ball with paint or with felt pieces glued on. The body of the puppet is made by draping a handkerchief over the hand. Rubber bands twisted around the third finger and thumb will hold the handkerchief securely in place and provide the puppet with two flexible arms.

A styrofoam ball may be used instead of a rubber ball to form a puppet head. It will be necessary to hollow out a depression in the foam large enough for the index finger to be inserted. Colored thumb tacks make suitable features for the styrofoam ball puppet.

Sock Puppets. A sock puppet is made by inserting an oval cardboard approximately five inches by three inches into the foot of the sock as an innersole. The cardboard should extend from the toe to the heel of the sock. The cardboard is then folded across the center, forming the upper and lower jaws of the puppet. When the puppeteer's hand is placed inside the sock with fingers above the top fold of the cardboard and thumb below the bottom fold, the puppet's mouth will open and close as the thumb and fingers are brought together. Features may be made with brads and scraps of colored paper or felt.

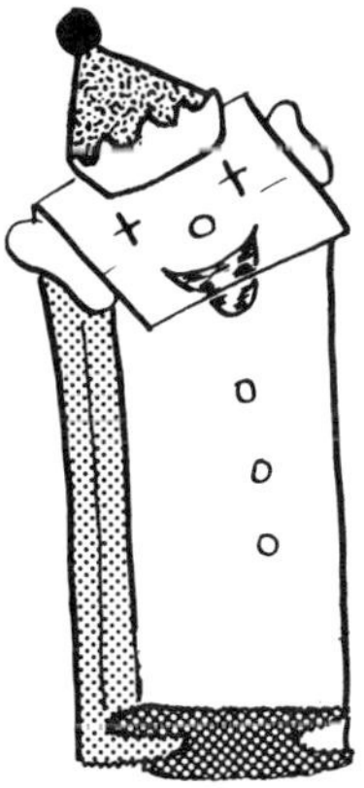
Fig. 3.4. Sack Puppet

Fig. 3.5. Rubber Ball Puppet

Fig. 3.6. Sock Puppet

Fig. 3.7. Box Puppet

Fig. 3.8. Vegetable Puppets

Fig. 3.9. These hand puppets of "Goldilocks and the Three Bears" were made by gluing a series of felt circles together and then attaching them to the toe of a sock.

Box Puppets. Box puppets are made by taping two small, deep boxes together with the openings of both boxes facing the puppeteer. A face is painted on the bottom of the two boxes with the mouth divided between the two. The upper half of the mouth goes on one box, and the lower half on the other. When the puppeteer's fingers are placed in the upper box and his thumb in the lower box, the puppet's mouth will open and close as the thumb and fingers are brought together.

Fruit and Vegetable Puppets. Puppets may be made from oranges, apples, pears, potatoes, carrots, and turnips by impaling the fruit or vegetable on a stick. (Children usually need help with this step.) Features for the puppet may be made of thumb tacks, brads, push pins, gold stars, and paper reinforcements.

The body of the fruit or vegetable puppet is made by inserting the stick through a small hole in the center of a handkerchief used to cover the puppeteer's hand. Fruit and vegetable puppets are, of course, perishable, but they will last for several days.

Cylinder Puppets. A cylinder puppet may be made by using a three-inch section cut from a paper towel tube. Hair, eyes, ears, nose, mouth, and clothing may be cut from felt or colored paper and glued in place on the cylinder. The puppet will move when the puppeteer's index and third fingers are placed inside the cylinder and bent forward.

Stick Puppets. The easiest of all puppets to construct and operate are the stick puppets. Pictures of people, animals, machines, furniture, and toys are cut from magazines. The shapes are glued on thin cardboard and cut out a second time. The stiffened shape is then taped to a stick or plastic drinking straw. The puppeteer grasps the stick and moves the puppet back and forth behind a screen. The audience sees only the body of the puppet above the screened area.

The art work of children may also be used to make very effective stick puppets.

Shadow Puppets. Shadow puppets for the overhead projector may be made by cutting silhouettes of storybook characters from black paper and taping them to a thin, stiff wire. By holding the wires, the puppeteer is able to move the shapes across the glass surface of the overhead projector without his hands being visible to the audience. The black paper blocks out the light and causes large images to appear on the screen.

Backgrounds for this type of shadow puppet may be made by drawing scenes on transparencies with colored felt point pens. Colored acetate may also be used effectively.

Fig. 3.10. Cylinder Puppet *Fig. 3.11.* Stick Puppet *Fig. 3.12.* Mask Puppet

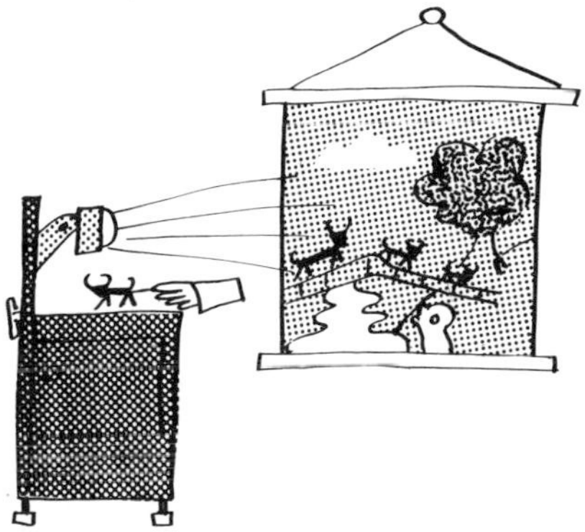

Fig. 3.13. Shadow Puppets

Fig. 3.14. Humanette Puppet

Fig. 3.15. These artistic humanette puppets were created by a group of boys and girls who designed them on the basis of information gained from *The First Book of Indians* by Benjamin Brewster. (Courtesy of West Hardin Independent School District, Sour Lake, Texas.)

Humanette Puppets. The humanette is a variation of the comical puppets used years ago to entertain vaudeville audiences. The humanette is a large cardboard cutout in the shape of a person, animal, plant, or machine. It is usually painted with tempera paints.

Openings are cut in the cardboard to allow the puppeteer's face and arms to come through. A finished humanette will fit children of all sizes, and may be used over and over to give all the children an opportunity to dramatize various character parts. No stage is needed.

Mask Puppets. Masks are made and worn by people to disguise, to transform, and to protect themselves. Children in the primary classroom usually make and wear masks to entertain themselves and others, yet they also can appreciate the fact that some people wear them for very serious reasons.

There is probably no exhibit easier to assemble than a display of masks, and none that provides more implications for cultural understanding. The ways in which masks are worn for protection by miners, firemen, skiers, welders, divers, motorcyclists, chemists, surgeons, and various other people makes a fascinating study for young children.

Practically any character from children's literature may be depicted by means of a simple, child-made mask. The easiest of all is made by stretching a nylon stocking over a wire coat hanger that has been slightly bent to form a face shape. Features are made by gluing felt, jewelry, buttons, or paper to the nylon. The puppeteer holds the mask in front of his face by grasping the hook of the coat hanger.

Regardless of the form it takes, dramatization as a reaction to literature should be much more than a parroted review of the content. It should result in elaboration, extension, and synthesis. One literature experience should be added to and compared with another so that children can understand why certain generalizations and principles predominate in every type of literature. If all experiences with books, magazines, and newspapers are integrated in such a way, children are much more likely to become critical, efficient consumers of literature, now and for the rest of their lives.

CHILDREN'S BOOKS FOR DRAMATIZATION

A, B, C: Go!, edited by Margaret E. Martignoni. New York: The Crowell-Collier Publishing Co., 1962. This collection of poems and stories for children is one of the "Collier's Junior Classics," a series of literature samplers. The volume is well illustrated with most of the art coming from the original works. It contains a total of 380 poems and stories by outstanding authors and poets.

Anatole and the Cat, written by Eve Titus and illustrated by Paul Galdone. New York: Whittlesey House, 1957. Anatole, the Cheese Taster, is the most honored and respected mouse in all of France. He also turns out to be the bravest by figuring out a way to do something that other mice had been talking about for thousands of years—a way to bell the cat!

The Bears on Hemlock Mountain, written by Alice Dalgliesh and illustrated by Helen Sewell, New York: Charles Scribner's Sons, 1952. Darkness overtakes Jonathan on Hemlock Mountain, where he was sent to borrow a large iron cooking pot from his Aunt Emma. When two bears block his path, Jonathan takes refuge under the big iron pot and stays there until help comes. Young readers are always amused and impressed by Jonathan's ingenuity.

Children's Literature for Dramatization: An Anthology, edited by Geraldine Brain Siks. New York: Harper & Row, Publishers, 1964. A collection of fifty-six stories and eighty-two poems chosen by the editor for their dramatic content. Many of the selections have been adapted for dramatic presentation. All the stories and poems were dramatized by children before being included in the collection.

Chimney Corner Stories, edited by Veronica S. Hutchinson and illustrated by Lois Lenski. New York: Minton, Balch & Co., 1925. This fine old collection contains sixteen of the world's most loved tales. It includes "The Three Billy Goats Gruff," "The Three Pigs," "The Pancake," "Henny Penny," and "The Little Red Hen and the Grain of Wheat."

Drummer Hoff, written by Barbara Emberley and illustrated by Ed Emberley. Englewood Cliffs, N. J.: Prentice-Hall, Inc., 1967. This is an adaptation of an old folk rhyme in which many people bring parts to assemble a cannon. Events accumulate until the cannon is finally fired—"Drummer Hoff fired it off." The rhyme ends abruptly as the cannon is fired. The last picture leaves the reader with a feeling of peace.

The Family Treasury of Children's Stories, Book I, edited by Pauline Rush Evans and illustrated by Donald Sibley. Garden City, N. Y.: Doubleday & Co., Inc., 1956. This book is a mammoth collection of some of the finest poems and stories that have ever been written for children. It begins with Mother Goose rhymes and the simplest stories for very young listeners.

Finders Keepers, written and illustrated by William Lipkind and Nicolas Mordvinoff. New York: Harcourt Brace Jovanovich, Inc., 1951. This is a story of two dogs who live together in peace and friendship until they find a bone. They ask all passersby to decide which of the two deserves to keep the bone. The ridiculous answers they get leave them no wiser. When they are forced to fight for the bone, they decide to share it.

The First Book of Indians, written by Benjamin Brewster and illustrated by Ursula Koering. New York: Franklin Watts, Inc., 1950. Benjamin Brewster, the author of this book, has been interested in Indians for many years. The book is authentic, factual and filled with accurate drawings and diagrams.

The Happy Lion, written by Louise Fatio and illustrated by Roger Duvoisin. New York: Whittlesey House, 1954. Everyone loves the happy lion so long as he is in the zoo surrounded by a moat, but when he escapes the zoo and strolls down the street, people behave differently. All in all he finds it best to be back in the zoo on the other side of the moat where people love him again.

Henry-Fisherman, written and illustrated by Marcia Brown. New York: Charles Scribner's Sons, 1949. Henry, a young boy living on an island in the Caribbean, wants more than anything to be a fisherman. When his father finally invites Henry to go out in the boat with him, exciting adventures ensue. This is a beautiful picture book that captures the beauty of a Caribbean island harbor "as safe as heaven itself."

Jeanne-Marie Counts Her Sheep, written and illustrated by Françoise. New York: Charles Scribner's Sons, 1951. Jeanne-Marie makes elaborate plans for all the things she will buy when her sheep Patapon has lambs. As she imagines more and more lambs, Jeanne Marie's list of wanted items grows. Eventually Patapon has one little lamb and there is just enough wool to knit Jeanne-Marie a pair of new socks. The story is illustrated with bright, poster-like pictures.

Little Tim and the Brave Sea Captain, written and illustrated by Edward Ardizzone. New York: Henry Z. Walck, Inc., 1955. Tim, a small boy who wants more than anything to be a sailor, stows away on an ocean steamer, He is forced to face storms, hard work, and other perils of being a sailor. Tim proves to be courageous and hardworking. He endears himself to the other sailors and especially to the captain, who finally sees Tim safely home again.

May I Bring a Friend?, written by Beatrice Schenk de Reginers and illustrated by Beni Montresor. New York: Atheneum, 1965. A young boy brings all his animal friends with him when he is invited to have tea with the king and queen. The animals return the hospitality by entertaining the king and queen with a tea at the city zoo. It is a delightfully humorous story told in verse form. It includes an informal presentation of the days of the week.

Mr. Penny, written and illustrated by Marie Hall Ets. New York: The Viking Press, 1935. Mr. Penny's large family of lazy farm animals keep him working long hours at the factory to keep them supplied with food. Finally, they have remorse and begin working together to make a fine garden for Mr. Penny. The garden provides funds for a new house, and Mr. Penny and his animals turn out to be "the happiest family in Wuddle."

Nora Kramer's Storybook, edited by Nora Kramer and illustrated by Beth and Joe Krush. New York: Gilbert Press, Inc., 1955. This book is an ample collection of stories and verse selected from contemporary literature. The material was chosen especially for children of ages three and four. Such writers as Kate Seredy, David McCord, and Munro Leaf are represented.

Once Upon A Time, edited by Rose Dobbs. New York: Random House, 1950. This is a collection of twenty old tales that have been favorites for storytelling over many years. Included are "The Half-Chick," "The Pine Tree," and "Clever Elsie." Many of the stories have been retold by the editor. They are very easy to prepare for storytelling.

Play With Me, written and illustrated by Marie Hall Ets. New York: The Viking Press, 1955. A little girl tries to capture small animals for companionship.

None of them will play with her. Finally, she sits very still and waits for them to come to her. An excellent book to show that pets need kindness, gentleness, and care.

Seven Diving Ducks, written by Margaret Friskey and illustrated by Jean Morey. New York: Children's Press, 1965. One little duckling in a family of seven is afraid to swim and dive. Father Duck is about to send him off to live with the chickens, when something happens that helps the timid little duck to be able to swim and dive as well as the others.

BIBLIOGRAPHY

Ackley, Edith Flack. *Marionettes*. Philadelphia, Pa.: J. B. Lippincott Co., 1929.

Ando, Tsuruo. *Bunraku, The Puppet Theatre*. New York: Walker-Weatherhill, 1970.

Arnott, Peter D. *Plays Without People*. Bloomington: Indiana University Press, 1964.

Baird, Bil. *The Art of the Puppet*. New York: The Macmillan Co., 1965.

Batchelder, Marjorie. *The Puppet Theatre Handbook*. New York: Harper & Row, Publishers, 1947.

Batchelder, Marjorie, and Comer, Virginia Lee. *Puppets and Plays*. New York: Harper & Row, Publishers, 1956.

Emberly, Ed. *Punch and Judy*. Boston: Little, Brown & Co., 1965.

Hunt, Kari, and Carlson, Bernice Wells. *Masks and Mask Makers*. New York: Abingdon Press, 1961.

Lewis, Roger. *Puppets and Marionettes*. New York: Alfred A. Knopf, Inc., 1952.

Lewis, Shari. *Making Easy Puppets*. New York: E. P. Dutton & Co., Inc., 1967.

Mattil, Edward L. *Meaning in Crafts*. Englewood Cliffs, N. J.: Prentice-Hall, Inc., 1971.

Rudolph, Marguerita, and Cohen, Dorothy H. *Kindergarten, A Year of Learning*. New York: Appleton-Century-Crofts, 1964.

Scott, A. C. *The Puppet Theatre of Japan*. Rutland, Vt.: Charles E. Tuttle Co., 1963.

Whitehead, Robert. *Children's Literature: Strategies of Teaching*. Englewood Cliffs, N. J.: Prentice-Hall, Inc., 1968.

4

"Talk Written Down—And More": Books and the Language Experience

That a child should read life before he reads books is a belief held by most teachers concerned with reading readiness and beginning reading. The skills of communication—oral language, listening, reading, and writing—begin in the home long before a child enters school. Moreover, a child's success in school may well depend on the quality and quantity of experiences he has encountered earlier. Only out of a reservoir of experiences is a fledgling reader able to bring meaning to the printed page. Unfortunately, many children have a limited backlog of experiences. The school is obligated to make up the deficit.

Numerous studies have shown the correlation between enriched learning experiences and success in reading. Conversely, the same studies serve to point up the relationship between a dearth of experiences and failure in reading. After studying the school records and interviewing the parents of 106 first graders, Almy concluded that there is a positive relationship between success in reading and such experiences as being read

1. Millie Corrine Almy, "Children's Experiences Prior to First Grade and Success in Beginning Reading," *Contributions to Education, No. 954* (New York: Bureau of Publications, Teachers College, Columbia University, 1949), p. 111.

to, looking at books and magazines, and an interest in words found on labels and signs.[1]

Lamoreaux and Lee maintain that readiness for reading depends on an accumulation of rich background experiences over a period of time:

> Our only means of understanding, of interpreting what we see and hear and feel, is through our own experience, real and vicarious. When a child's background of experience is so limited that he can find in it no basis for interpreting the material he reads, it will have no more meaning for him than highly technical material in an unfamiliar field would for us.[2]

Esther Milner's study completed a few years later, corroborated their opinion.[3] She compared the achievement of children from middle-class homes with that of children from lower-class homes and found that the child from a middle-class home had a definite verbal advantage and was therefore better equipped for reading. She attributed the differential to experiences provided in the middle-class home.

Many writers have been concerned with providing compensatory experiences in the classroom for those students who lack the necessary generalizations and understandings by which a reader brings meaning to the printed page. Harris describes the need for teachers to provide vicarious experiences in the classroom for such students:

> If a child has never seen a horse, and if his teacher finds it inconvenient to take him to a farm, a photograph or drawing will substitute for the actual experience. A geography teacher usually cannot take his class on a surveying trip to Colorado, but a good map will tell the students more about the state's geography than a thousand words. It may not be practical to dismantle a jet engine in a classroom, but drawings and diagrams are more effective substitutes than a fat and wordy textbook.[4]

Trauger stresses that all teachers should know why they seek out interesting concrete materials of various kinds to help students enlarge and enrich their accumulation of experiences:

> A teacher's search for audiovisual possibilities may correct the prevalent inclination to talk too much and too abstractly. Language arts classes tend to be overwordy—a tendency prompted by the nature

2. Lillian A. Lamoreaux and Dorris May Lee, *Learning to Read Through Experience* (New York: Appleton-Century-Crofts, 1943), p. 5.

3. Esther Milner, "A Study of the Relationship Between Reading Readiness in Grade One School Children and Patterns of Parent-Child Interactions," *Child Development* 22 (1951):95-112.

4. Ben M. Harris, *Supervisory Behavior in Education* (Englewood Cliffs, N. J.: Prentice-Hall, Inc., 1963), p. 303.

Fig. 4.1. The book, *Pelle's New Suit* means a great deal to students of this school as they help shear a sheep they have raised. The barn in the background was built by parents and teachers. (Courtesy of Saint Thomas Episcopal School, College Station, Texas.)

of the subject. Use of graphic materials reduces abstractness and excessive talk.[5]

Strickland also strongly emphasizes the need for all kinds of learning experiences with audiovisual aids, to be supplied by the school in a planned and routine fashion:

> Firsthand and vicarious experiences are both essential to language development. Field trips, experimentation, and various types of individual exploration are used where they prove valuable. Reading and audiovisual materials supply vicarious experiences.[6]

The National Council of Teachers of English has long urged teachers to meet the diverse needs of students by providing them with interesting, challenging experiences that demand involvement and participation:

> Planning individual and group projects and making contacts with resource persons are challenging experiences through which young

5. Wilma K. Trauger, *Language Arts in Elementary Schools* (New York: McGraw-Hill Book Co., 1963), p. 8.
6. Ruth G. Strickland, *The Language Arts in the Elementary School* (New York: D. C. Heath and Co., 1963), p. 61.

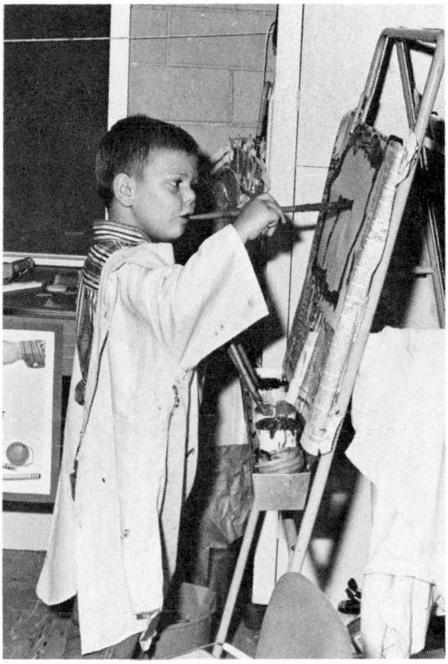

Fig. 4.2. One of the most effective ways to give students ample opportunity for personal expression to books and stories is to provide an easel with tempera paint, and large, soft brushes. (Courtesy of South Park Independent School District, Beaumont, Texas.)

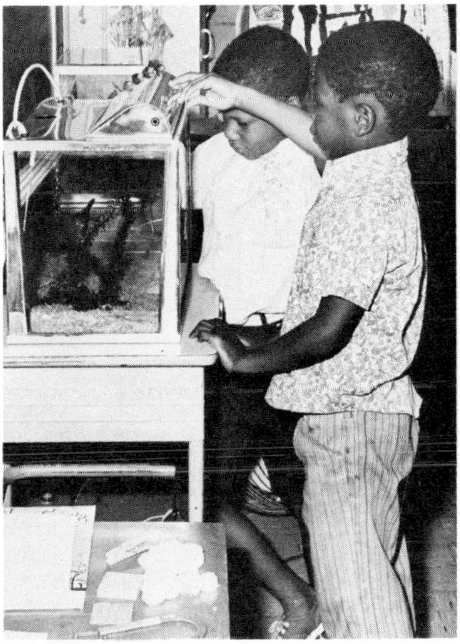

Fig. 4.3. Children's personal observations and discoveries lead to enriched oral and written language. (Courtesy of South Park Independent School District, Beaumont, Texas.)

people gain competence in observing, thinking, speaking, listening, reading, and writing. Such planning is one means of individualizing goals, procedures, materials, and evaluation. Sharing the results of individual and small group projects can socialize individual talent and achievement.[7]

Bernard records the psychological bases for drawing on a child's own experiences to teach him the various language skills:

> Meaning always has reference to the individual and it is derived from his own experiences. The pupil must touch, feel, taste, see, hear, and manipulate objects in his environment in order to understand them. As he shifts from the world of objects to the realm of words, which represent objects and situations, he must make the transition in progressive steps. Meanings, to a great extent, actually constitute

7. National Council of Teachers of English, *The English Language Arts* (New York: Appleton-Century-Crofts, 1952), p. 257.

the environment of the individual—especially his psychological environment.[8]

John Dewey was concerned with the *quality* of the experiences provided children, and consistently emphasized the need for "carry over" value in the experiences offered: "The more definitely and sincerely it is held that education is a development within, by, and for experience, the more important it is that there shall be clear conceptions of what experience is."[9] Dewey held that each experience should be of the quality to bring forth other fruitful experiences in the future.

Burton and his collaborators see as did Dewey, the importance of quality in the experiences planned and arranged for children, and advocate activities that would lead to inquiry and problem solving:

> The teacher must respect and keep alive the poking of little children from which knowledge results. Inquisitiveness, asking others, must be encouraged and stimulated until it becomes the ability to find out things for oneself, ability to "think up" new hypotheses to be followed. The school must lead "curiosity" over into vital problem solving and more critical inquiry which constitutes thinking.[10]

Lee and Allen take a slightly different approach in their writing about experiences and their implications for learning. They see the experience curriculum as the logical and necessary one to employ in a society that claims to be free and democratic:

> The reading program which is based on the learner's experience should reflect the goals of a society which values creativity and divergent thinking. Learning experiences are selected which generate productive thinking, allow freedom of expression, stimulate individuality, value ingenuity, satisfy curiosity and promote personal satisfaction to the extent that learning to read is a lifelong experience which requires ever maturing and more complex skills and knowledge.[11]

From extensive studies with economically deprived children, Frost concluded that a restricted vocabulary produces a restricted reader. He urged the school to provide young children with a systematic program of linguistic development beginning with each child's previous experiences:

8. Harold W. Bernard, *Psychology of Learning and Teaching* (New York: McGraw-Hill Book Co., 1954), p. 34.

9. John Dewey, *Experience and Education* (New York: The Macmillan Co., 1938), p. 17.

10. William H. Burton, Roland B. Kimball, and Richard L. Wigg, *Education for Effective Thinking* (New York: Appleton-Century-Crofts, 1960), p. 339.

11. Dorris M. Lee and R. V. Allen, *Learning to Read Through Experience* (New York: Appleton-Century-Crofts, 1963), p. 13.

> These related concepts that the child has programmed in his cognitive structure are the basis for all intelligent functions and impose boundaries for the child's progress in school. These meanings, brought to school by the child, have been shaped by the nature and quality of living with others, and they may be intensified and broadened through environmental enrichment or they may be restricted by depriving the child of multiple opportunities to use his avenues of learning—the senses—in rich meaningful ways.[12]

More and more concerned people in and outside the teaching profession are beginning to realize that the responsibility of providing children with the experiences necessary for success in school rests, in large measure, with the school itself, and cannot be relegated entirely to the home and community. According to Smith and Dechant:

> If the child's environment fails to stimulate perceptual growth, the school must attempt to provide the necessary experiences. This implies that we should be particularly eager to supply stimulating nursery school and kindergarten experiences as well as such physical experiences as neighborhood reading centers, bookmobiles, group trips, and day-camp organizations to children from the lower socio-economic groups. The provision of these opportunities for cultural experiences has long been recognized as a social responsibility of the community. It may be that it is even more precisely an educational responsibility.[13]

Even a brief survey of the literature reveals a consensus among child development specialists, curriculum planners, and language authorities that young children need stimulating work centers, rich play activities, ample space, movable furniture, good classroom libraries, and quantities of raw materials for work. The present problem is one of finding ways to implement the results of the studies and of using the knowledge such studies have contributed to the area of early childhood education.

Experience Charts

Learning to read through experience is based on the premise that a reader recognizes printed symbols and endows them with meaning. Meaning comes from within the reader rather than from the reading material. A dramatic episode in the life of Helen Keller describes her sudden discovery that printed words are representations of language:

12. Joe L. Frost, *Early Childhood Education Rediscovered* (New York: Holt, Rinehart & Winston, Inc., 1968), p. 382.

13. Henry P. Smith and Emerald V. Dechant, *Psychology in Teaching Reading* (Englewood Cliffs, N. J.: Prentice-Hall, Inc., 1961), p. 98.

Fig. 4.4. Two nursery school children transfer chicks from the incubator to a brooder. Under the teacher's guidance, the class built the incubator and tended the eggs until they hatched. *All About Eggs and How They Turn into Animals* by Millicent Selsam was used as resource material. Directions for making a classroom incubator may be found in Appendix B. (Courtesy of Concord Day School, Beaumont, Texas.)

> We walked down the path to the well-house, attracted by the fragrance of the honeysuckle with which it was covered. Someone was drawing water and my teacher placed my hand under the spout. As the cool stream gushed over one hand she spelled into the other the word *water,* first slowly, then rapidly. I stood still, my whole attention fixed upon the motions of her fingers. Suddenly I felt a misty consciousness as of something forgotten—a thrill of returning thought; and somehow the mystery of language was revealed to me. I knew then that "W-A-T-E-R" meant the wonderful cool something that was flowing over my hand. That living word awakened my soul, gave it light, hope, joy, set it free![14]

Something akin to that experience of Helen Keller's happens to young children who are permitted to observe their own experiences recorded in print and then read back to them.

The experience chart is the most effective means by which to help a child conceptualize what reading is—speech written down—and more. It also serves to capture an experience in permanent form and provides highly interesting reading material for the classroom.

14. Helen Keller, *The Story of My Life* (Garden City, N. Y.: Doubleday & Co., Inc., 1920), pp. 23-24.

If the experience has been a shared one, the teacher and children can usually produce the chart story cooperatively, with the teacher serving as secretary or recorder to get the children's ideas down on paper. If the experience has been a personal one, the teacher may wish to help the child compose an individual chart story. In either case, the chart is a joint enterprise growing out of an experience that is happening at the present time, has happened in the recent past, or is to take place in the near future. In other words, the teacher does not compose a chart for children in their absence, present it to them for reading, and then perhaps store it for use with a new group of students. Such a chart might have a worthy purpose, but it would be a misnomer to label it an *experience* chart.

Lee and Allen have outlined five major principles for guiding teachers in the use of language experience stories:

1. What a child thinks about, he can talk about.
2. What one talks about can be expressed in writing.
3. Anything the teacher or child writes can be read.
4. One can read what he writes and what other people write.
5. What a child has to say is as important to him as what other people have written for him to read.[15]

Composing the Experience Chart

When an experience has been interesting enough to stimulate discussion by the children, the teacher should be prepared to record key comments and ideas on chart paper, making an effort to write the chart sentences in the child's own language. Any radical departure from a child's original contribution is apt to cause him to be skeptical of the entire process. If the teacher feels the need to make a change in the content or structure of a child's contribution, the change should be carefully explained to the child and made only on his approval. No honest effort of a child to express himself in art, in writing, or in oral language should be altered by the "touch of the master's hand" to the point it is no longer the child's creation.

Sources of Experiences

Many experiences suitable for chart making are spontaneous classroom situations, and a perceptive teacher is continually alert to the value

15. Lee and Allen, op. cit., p. 46.

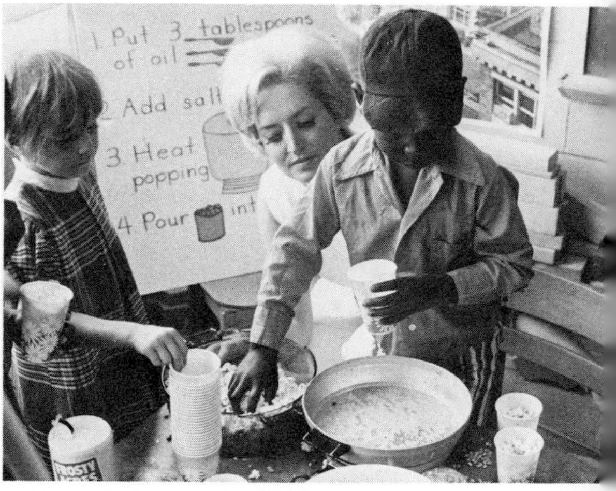

Fig. 4.5. Systematic analysis and evaluation of experiences are necessary if objectives of the experience approach are to be attained. (Courtesy of South Park Independent School District, Beaumont, Texas.)

of such windfalls. But teaching cannot depend on serendipity and it becomes necessary to plan and initiate experiences on a routine basis. Any teacher who knows well the interests and abilities of the children, and their readiness for a particular activity, can become skillful at creating happenings guaranteed to give them something to think about, talk about, read and write about.

Fig. 4.6. This girl is taking pictures of an Indian village constructed by her classmates. The photographs will provide a record of the experience for future use in chart making and creative writing. (Courtesy of West Hardin Independent School District, Sour Lake, Texas.)

Systematic analysis and evaluation of experiences are necessary if objectives of the experience approach are to be attained. This includes making careful notes of the conversation and comments made by children during an experience. It may also include the use of tape recordings, Polaroid snapshots, and other methods of recording reactions.

A teacher aide is invaluable in the task of recording an experience, and with supervision and practice, can learn to observe, record, and retrieve the most important elements of the experience. The teacher, of course, is occupied during this time as a catalyst in making significant things happen, in asking leading questions, and in clarifying concepts. Graphic records produced by such a team effort not only provide a means of appraisal, but are also raw material for language experience chart making.

Books and the Language Experience

Children's literature is a ubiquitious source of rich language experience for children. Books are always ready and available when other experience sources, such as a field trip or resource person, are impractical at the moment. Books obviously do not substitute for real life experiences, but they add to the richness of a firsthand experience, and they can also provide some of the vicarious experiences necessary in a child's life.

When children have been introduced to such interesting and entertaining books as *The Five Chinese Brothers, Where the Wild Things Are, The Crows of Pear Blossom,* or *Many Moons,* the natural outcome is lively discussion. And from the flow of oral language, experience charts are developed. Effective uses of such literature charts over a period of time help young children to develop positive attitudes toward books and reading.

Authors, librarians, illustrators of children's books, teachers of literature, book sellers, storytellers, and other bibliophiles make excellent resource people for the classroom, not only because they recognize children as consumers of their product, but also because most of them genuinely like to talk about books—especially to such avid fans as young children. Charts may be developed in planning the visit, in recording the interaction between the visitor and children, and in a follow-up summary of the visit. Other language experiences to be gleaned from literature might include the purchase of a needed book, the arrival of a shipment of paperbacks, a comparative study of two popular books, construction of a literature bulletin board, a study of illustrations, and a reorganization of the classroom collection.

The following brief list offers additional possibilities for rich language experiences:

- Resource persons
- Field trips
- Creative dramatics
- Storytelling
- Puppetry
- Creative writing
- Experiments
- Work sessions
- Dramatic play
- Discussions and conversations
- Art activities
- Cooking
- Celebrations and holidays
- "Show and tell"
- Outdoor play
- Films and film strips
- Slides and transparencies
- Pictures and art prints
- Advertisements
- Travel posters
- Objects and models
- Pets and animals

Chart Making

If language experience charts are to be employed as an integral part of the reading and reading readiness programs, it is imperative that both

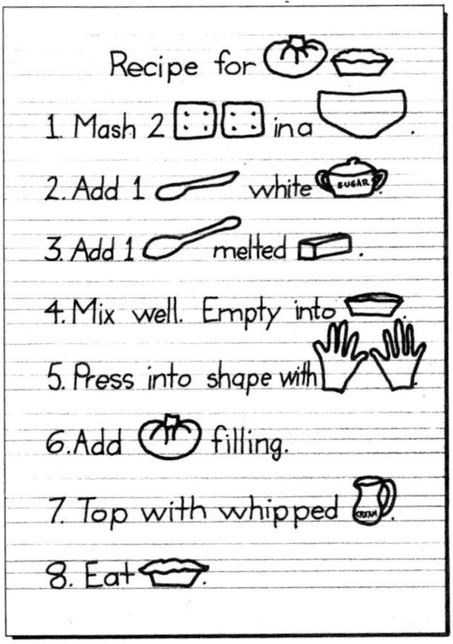

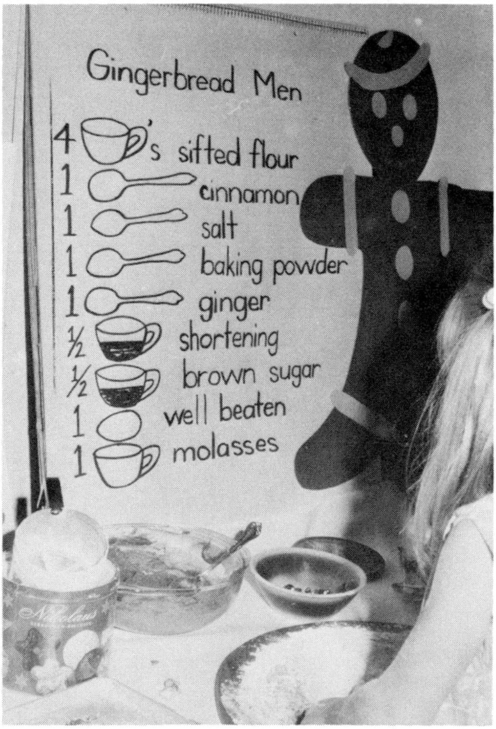

Figs. 4.7 and 4.8. Rebus pictures make a recipe chart easy to read and follow. Reviewing the recipe chart can help children to see that writing is a way of recording information for future reference.

the teacher and aide be able to make them quickly, efficiently, and fluently. Tedious and laborious efforts are certain to cause a loss of interest among the children who are observing and participating in the chart's development. At the same time, the finished chart should be attractive, well balanced, and above all, legible. Only with much practice on the spot in the classroom can the skill of chart making be fully attained.

Since language experience charts are to serve as a transition between oral language and reading, they should resemble as closely as possible the printed page. The writing should be done in manuscript form with black ink on white paper. Chart papers range from newsprint to the more expensive lined tagboard. The purpose and intended uses of the chart determine the degree of permanency desired. A chart that proves to be better than average may always be transferred to a better quality paper. Materials needed for chart making include:

- Chart tablets
    - 24″ x 16″ (easel style)
    - 24″ x 32″ (full length)
- Sentence strips and rolls
- Pocket chart
- Chart paper
- Primary typewriter
- Felt point pens
- Water base pens for children's use
- Crayons
- Pictures
- Scissors and paste
- Manuscript alphabet guide

The want ad section and stock market page of the daily newspaper make excellent material for practicing manuscript writing. If the paper is turned crosswise, the columns provide lines and spaces of the correct size for writing.

Illustrating the Experience Chart

Any chart that is to be used several times with a group of children deserves to be illustrated either by the children or by the teacher. Appropriate illustrations, such as pictures in books, add color and emphasis to the printed material and make it much more appealing and understandable to children. However, no chart should become cluttered with pictures. Illustrations are meant to enhance the writing and not detract from it. The following list offers sources of materials to use in illustrating experience charts:

Painting and drawings made by the students
Paintings and drawings made by the teacher or aide
Art prints
Magazine pictures
Photographs
Rebus drawings
Book jackets
Travel folders
Worn-out picture books.
Illustrations from workbooks
Old readiness books
Illustrations from sales catalogues, stamp books, and seed catalogues.

Using the Experience Chart

Although the language experience approach is seldom used as the sole method of teaching reading, it is considered by most reading specialists to be an excellent vehicle for humanizing and personalizing the reading program.

Authorities hesitate to recommend the experience approach as a total program for fear that the systematic teaching of reading skills might be neglected. Heilman is one of the writers in the field of reading who has reservations about using the language experience chart as a total program. He believes that the method should be a supplement to other materials designed to teach reading skills:

> Most teachers prefer to use the experience chart as a supplement to basals and other materials. This permits certain of the weaknesses to be minimized. The basic readers provide drill on sight vocabulary and control over the introduction of new words. The use of experience charts add flexibility and interest to the program.[16]

Perhaps it would be risky to use experience charts as a total method, but it certainly is a misconception to assume that charts do *not* teach reading skills. A well-made reading chart, arising out of a significant experience, makes reading personal and relevant: it also strengthens and reinforces the skills of reading. To dichotomize the issue is a waste of time and energy. Both teacher-made and commercial reading materials have a place in the classroom.

16. Arthur W. Heilman, *Principles and Practices of Teaching Reading*, 3rd ed. (Columbus, Ohio: Charles E. Merrill Publishers, 1972), p. 211.

The greatest strength of the experience chart is its appeal for children. Because of the ego involvement inherent in formulating a chart, children are immediately attracted to it. It is not difficult to understand why. Charts employ the names of the children, and the names of their friends, relatives, and acquaintances. They make use of the names of plants, animals, machines, toys, buildings, cities, foods, holidays, celebrations, and other words of high appeal to children. Fortunately, they also employ an abundance of service words needed to tie the more colorful and interesting words together. In fact, an experience chart is one of the most palatable ways to give children the necessary multiple exposures to service words.

If the experience chart is to be considered a springboard for skill activities, as well as a means of creating interest in reading, teachers and aides need to know a variety of chart types. The following list offers some of the major initial uses of a chart:

To illustrate how speech can be recorded in print
Review an experience
Present new information
Provide oral and silent reading practice

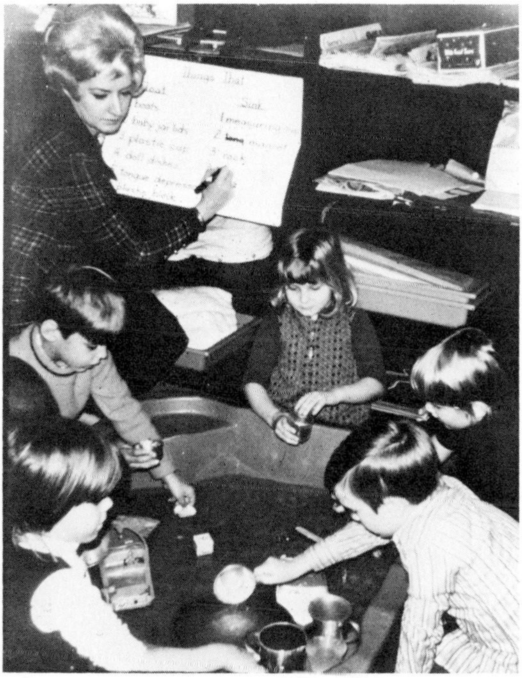

Fig. 4.9. Children test out hypotheses as the teacher records their findings on a chart. (Courtesy of Deer Park Independent School District, Deer Park, Texas.)

Form a base for discussion
Enlarge and enrich vocabulary
Give directions
List criteria
State hypotheses
Record a happening
Summarize learnings
Initiate a project
Celebrate an occasion
Reinforce skills
Promote creative writing
Provide reference material
Evaluate an activity
Dramatize a book or an event

Follow-up cases for charts are just as numerous as the teacher's imagination and ingenuity will allow. Some of the more obvious uses of a chart that has served its initial purpose are given below:

1. The chart may be cut into sentences and reassembled to give practice in sequence.

2. The chart may provide practice on the word attack skills—phonetic analysis, context clues, and structural analysis.

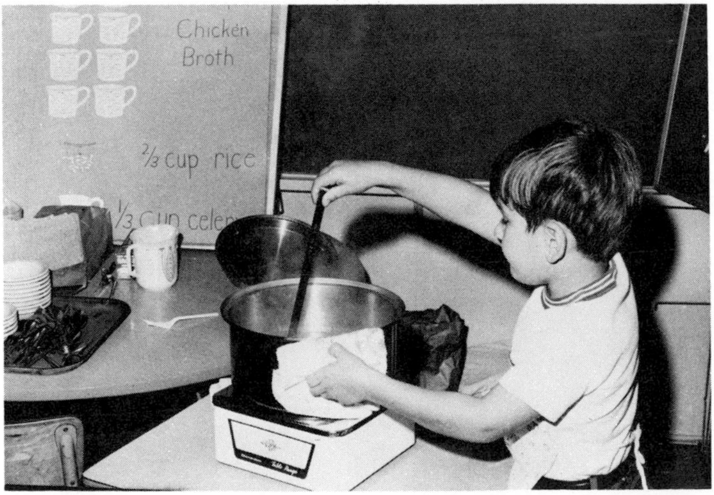

Fig. 4.10. A recipe chart may provide new words for vocabulary building and teach fractions at the same time. (Courtesy of South Park Independent School District, Beaumont, Texas.)

3. The chart may be used to review capitalization, punctuation, and sentence structure.

4. Several charts may be bound together to make an oversized book of stories for the reading table.

5. Chart stories may be transcribed on the primary typewriter to make small booklets for the reading table.

6. Charts and booklets may be exchanged with other classes to provide more practice in silent reading.

7. Dated charts may be sent home for children to read to parents.

8. Some charts may be cut up to make dictionary boxes and word games.

Creative Writing and the Language Experience

As children come to know the joy of seeing their own thoughts and ideas recorded in print, they soon feel the need to do some of their own writing. It is a short step from the dictated story to one which a child writes for himself. In watching the teacher record his speech, the child has learned something about letter formation, spelling, sentence structure, punctuation, and other elements of writing. With a great deal of help and encouragement, he is able to use the mechanics of writing to express his own thoughts and feelings.

Writing is creative when a child gives an honest and sincere response to the world around him, and then is able to capture that response in writing. Essential mechanics of writing are necessary tools for recording responses, but rules and techniques are never more important than the expression itself. In beginning writing, the emphasis must always be on freedom of expression.

Years ago, Alvina Burrows and her colleagues conducted exhaustive experiments in which they attempted to release free expression from children while cultivating the skill necessary for writing with correctness and ease. They arrived at the following conclusion, which might well serve as a guide for today's teachers of language arts:

> We know that if a child is to be an effective, poised personality, he must have an awareness and an appreciation of his own power. Such self-knowledge comes only through frequent opportunity to experiment and to fumble along the lines of his desire until out of his effort he fashions something which in his eyes is good. That the product is often crude and clumsy does not matter. The important thing is that the child, out of himself and working in his own way, has produced a thing of which he can approve.[17]

17. Alvina Treut Burrows et al., *They All Want to Write* (Englewood Cliffs, N. J.: Prentice-Hall, Inc., 1952), pp. 1-2.

The Teacher of Creative Writing

An inspiring teacher is the key to creative writing. It is the teacher's responsibility to maintain a relaxed and accepting environment, to provide many ideas and topics for writing, to give needed help with composition, and to make wise use of the finished products. Above all, the teacher must be encouraging. Nothing squelches the urge to write like a disapproving teacher. A harshly critical word at a crucial moment can cause a child to become overly cautious and less creative in future attempts. An understanding teacher realizes that the young writer's ideas are fragile and vulnerable, and respects them accordingly.

Maintaining an environment where creativity can flourish, and giving children many opportunities for self-expression are vital to creative writing. These two practices alone, however, are not the sole answer. Creative writing must be systematically and routinely taught. Petty and Bowen give a convincing argument that creative writing be taught much like the other creative arts:

> We say that it really *can* be taught—just as the other creative arts are—but it must be *taught*. While it is true that some painters, musicians, or dancers are innately talented and have received little teaching, the majority of persons engaged in these arts, professionally or simply for enjoyment, have received instruction—they have been *taught*.[18]

Those teachers who are successful in the teaching of creative writing seem to have certain characteristics in common. They are sensitive to their students' needs and interests. They are tolerant of their students' awkwardness, and more generous in the appraisal of their efforts. They genuinely appreciate and respect the language of children with its straightforward frankness.

Lowenfeld and Brittain have found that whatever a teacher does in stimulating creativeness greatly depends on three factors: his own personality, of which his own creativeness, his degree of sensitivity, and flexible relationships to environment are an important part; his ability to put himself into the place of others; his understanding and knowledge of the needs of those whom he is teaching.[19]

Herbert Kohl, the author of *36 Children*, is a staunch advocate of creative writing in the classroom as a means of improving the self-image of students. He believes that if children are encouraged by teachers to dis-

18. Walter T. Petty and Mary E. Bowen, *Slithery Snakes and Other Aids to Children's Writing* (New York: Appleton-Century-Crofts, 1967), pp. 4-5.

19. Viktor Lowenfeld and W. Lambert Brittain, *Creative and Mental Growth*, 4th ed. (New York: The Macmillan Co., 1964), p. 11.

cover themselves in the classroom, they will not need to resort to self-discovery on the streets and through drugs. After many attempts to free children of the self-doubt that inhibits expression, Kohl wrote:

> It is absurd that young people fear their own writing and are ashamed of their own voices. We have to encourage them to listen to themselves and each other, and to take the time to discover who they are for themselves. If teachers respect the voices of the young, and nurture them instead of tearing them down or trying to develop ones for students, then perhaps school will be less oppressive and alienating to the young.[20]

Fortunately, very young children have not become so self-conscious about expressing themselves and, for the most part, are anxious to write. They see writing as a fascinating extension of their own speech. Once they have attained the rudimentary skills of writing, have something to say and a reason for saying it, they write willingly and freely.

Literature and Creative Writing

As in the case of experience chart making, stimulating experiences with children's literature are among the best sources of input for creative writing. They provide the inspiration and raw material for letters, stories, poems, plays, and reports.

Literature read aloud to children in the classroom brings forth all manner of creative expression. If the teacher reads "The Elephant's Child" from Kipling's *Just So Stories,* some children may immediately make drawings and paintings of the bi-colored python rock snake. Moreover, they are often stimulated to create excellent "why" stories of their own.

If the teacher shares unrhymed poetry with the children, they may want to try their hand at it—even if only a line or two. Their poems may be transferred to newsprint to be used as reading charts, and eventually taken home for parents to enjoy.

Animal stories read aloud by the teacher or aide trigger memories of all kinds of experiences children have had with pets and animals, and original stories are often the result. Such stories make excellent reading material if they are illustrated, bound together, and placed on the library table.

Such books as *The Cow Who Fell in the Canal, Harry the Dirty Dog,* and *Five-O'Clock Charlie* show animals in humorous situations and give

20. Herbert Kohl, "Writing Their Way to Self-Acceptance," *Grade Teacher* 87 (1969):9-11.

children a starting point for their own stories about wise and foolish animals.

The correlation between literature and creative activities is endless. The teacher only needs to know ways of bringing the two together. Listed below are a dozen double-purpose activities for the promotion of both literature and creative writing:

1. Writing personal reactions to books that are read aloud by the teacher or aide at storytime. Bind reactions together into a book for the library table.

2. Making new book jackets for favorite books. Use any art process desired to decorate the jacket and then write a blurb that will advertise the book. Write a continuation of the blurb containing a biographical sketch of the author.

3. Compiling a scrapbook of brief book reviews written by children. Let it serve as a source of information to young browsers.

4. Writing a set of provocative questions about books that have circulated in the class. The questions are then compiled into a literary quiz program for the class.

5. Writing letters to the librarian requesting purchase of books that follow interests of class members. Such books might include information on hobbies, collections, sports, or pets. Explain why such books are needed.

6. Writing comparative essays in which one book is compared to another. Other comparisons might include authors, illustrators, or book characters.

7. Writing additional adventures to a book that is made up of episodes such as *Hitty: Her First Hundred Years, Homer Price, My Father's Dragon, Pippi Longstocking,* or *Amelia Bedelia.*

8. Writing a letter to parents explaining why a certain book is wanted as a Christmas or birthday gift.

9. Writing a letter to a classmate recommending a certain book. Justify the recommendation with valid arguments for the book's merit.

10. Writing an essay explaining why a certain book deserved to win the Caldecott Award.

11. Writing a new ending to an old favorite such as *The Pied Piper of Hamelin, Miss Hickory,* or *Down, Down the Mountain.*

12. Writing an imaginary letter to a well-known book character, or an imaginery conversation between two characters.

Teaching reading as a language experience is based on the belief that children learn to read more effectively and take greater pleasure in the process when they help to compose their own literature, when they have the privilege of reading back their own words and thoughts that have been recorded in printed form. Not only do they have a good time with the reading experience, but they also strengthen and refine the skills of reading at the same time. In making and re-reading an experience chart, children gain practice in the skills of phonetic analysis, structural analysis, contextual clues, and configuration. Thus, spanning the distance between oral and written language, experience charts become the perfect literature for the pre-reader and the beginning reader.

CHILDREN'S BOOKS FOR LANGUAGE EXPERIENCES

All About Eggs and How They Change Into Animals, written by Millicent Selsam and illustrated by Helen Ludwig. New York: William R. Scott, Inc., 1952. A science book of factual information that is interesting enough to hold the attention of young children and simple enough for them to understand. The story of eggs begins with the most familiar of all, the egg of a hen. It ends with a description and an illustration of the egg that grows inside a human mother.

The Cow Who Fell in the Canal, written by Phyllis Krasilovsky and illustrated by Peter Spier. Garden City, N. Y.: Doubleday & Co., Inc., 1957. Hendrika, a faithful milk cow, lives on a farm in Holland, but she is bored with eating and eating and eating. One day she falls into the canal and onto a raft. The raft floats downstream to a city. There Hendrika sees so many interesting sights that she stores up enough memories to keep her entertained the rest of her life on the farm.

Down, Down the Mountain, written and illustrated by Ellis Credle. New York: Thomas Nelson and Sons, 1934. Hetty and Hank, who live in a little log cabin in the Blue Ridge Mountains, want new shoes to wear to church on Sunday. Their granny tells them to plant turnip seeds and trade the turnips for shoes. This plan brings many adventures to Hetty and Hank. Eventually they take their fine big turnips down to the town at the foot of the mountain.

Five O'Clock Charlie, written by Marguerite Henry and illustrated by Wesley Dennis. New York: Rand McNally & Co., 1962. Based on a true incident, as are all of Marguerite Henry's horse stories, *Five O'Clock Charlie* is the story of an endearing old work horse who refuses to accept retirement with its life of ease—and boredom. Charlie finds a way "to make his loneliness vanish like a fog when the sun comes out." Most horse stories are too difficult for young readers. This one is an exception.

Hitty: Her First Hundred Years, written by Rachel Field and illustrated by Dorothy Lathrop. New York: The Macmillan Co., 1930. Hitty, a small antique wooden doll carved from mountain ash wood, writes her memoirs over a period of a hundred years. Hitty's thrilling adventures take her across the United States and to foreign countries. The story was actually inspired by a doll the author and illustrator purchased years ago from an antique shop in New York City.

Homer Price, written and illustrated by Robert McCloskey. New York: The Viking Press, 1943. Six tales of riotous laughter are built around the escapades of a typical adolescent boy. All the characters with whom Homer Price has dealings are memorable and very much like our own neighbors. The book is extremely popular with boys.

Just So Stories, written and illustrated by Rudyard Kipling. Garden City, N. Y.: Doubleday & Co., Inc., 1907. These long popular "why" stories tell how the various animals came to be. Similar to ancient folk tales, each story is pure fun and nonsense balanced with the right amount of realism. The stories are excellent for the teacher or aide to read aloud because of the rich vocabulary and rhythmic style. For smooth reading, the stories should be practiced in advance.

Many Moons, written by James Thurber and illustrated by Louis Slobodkin. New York: Harcourt, Brace Jovanovich, Inc., 1943. The story of how a little princess named Lenore asks for the moon and gets it. When all the Royal Wise Men have tried and failed to capture the elusive moon, Lenore and her friend, the Court Jester, devise a plan that works. A delightful fantasy for eight- and nine-year-olds.

Miss Hickory, written by Carolyn Sherwin Bailey and illustrated by Ruth Gannett. New York: The Viking Press, 1946. Miss Hickory is a doll made from an applewood twig with a hickory nut head. She lives in a corncrib house under a lilac bush. This story of fantasy tells how Miss Hickory lives among neighbors like Crow, Bull Frog, Ground Hog, and Squirrel. The surprise ending to the book teaches a subtle lesson on hope and immortality.

My Father's Dragon, written by Ruth Stiles Gannett and illustrated by Ruth Chrisman Gannett. New York: Random House, 1948. A young boy rescues the baby dragon from his tormenters by outwitting the wild animals who are using the dragon as a ferryboat to cross the river. A humorous adventure story of danger and daring. Chapter titles such as "My Father Meets a Lion" and "My Father Meets a Gorilla" appeal to young readers and listeners.

Pelle's New Suit, written and illustrated by Elsa Beskow. New York: Harper & Row, Publishers, 1929. In this realistic story from Sweden, a small boy earns his new suit by raising his own sheep. After shearing the sheep, Pelle takes the wool to be carded, spun into yarn, woven into cloth, dyed, and sewn into a suit. It is a simplified, entertaining story of how woolen cloth is made. Beautiful illustrations make it easy for young children to follow the sequential steps.

Pippi Longstocking, written by Astrid Lindgren and illustrated by Louis S. Glanzman. New York: The Viking Press, 1950. Pippi Longstocking is one of the most hilarious characters in children's literature. She is a little orphan girl who lives alone except for her pets, and has the privilege of doing exactly as she pleases. She keeps telling everyone, "Don't worry about me. I'll come out on top." Indeed she does. Young readers envy her carefree existence.

BIBLIOGRAPHY

Almy, Millie Corine. "Children's Experiences Prior to First Grade and Success in Beginning Reading." *Contributions to Education,* No. 954. New York: Bureau of Publications, Teachers College, Columbia University, 1949.

Applegate, Mauree. *Easy in English.* New York: Harper & Row, Publishers, 1960.

———. *Freeing Children to Write.* New York: Harper & Row, Publishers, 1963.

Bernard, Harold W. *Psychology of Learning and Teaching.* New York: McGraw-Hill Book Co., 1954.

Burrows, Alvina Treut, Ferebee, June D.; Jackson, Doris C.; Saunders, Dorothy O. *They All Want to Write.* New York: Prentice-Hall, Inc., 1952.

Burton, William H.; Kimball, Roland B.; Wigg, Richard L. *Education for Effective Thinking.* New York: Appleton-Century-Crofts, 1960.

Frost, Joe L. *Early Childhood Education Rediscovered.* New York: Holt, Rinehart & Winston, Inc., 1968.

Hall, Mary Anne. *Teaching Reading as a Language Experience.* Columbus, Ohio: Charles E. Merrill Publishers, 1970.

Harris, Ben M. *Supervisory Behavior in Education.* Englewood Cliffs, N. J.: Prentice-Hall, Inc., 1963.

Heilman, Arthur W. *Principles and Practices of Teaching Reading.* 2nd ed., Columbus, Ohio: Charles E. Merrill Publishers, 1961.

Herrick, Virgil E., and Marcella Nerbovig. *Using Experience Charts with Children.* Columbus, Ohio: Charles E. Merrill Publishers, 1964.

Keller, Helen. *The Story of My Life.* Garden City: Doubleday & Co., 1920.

Kohl, Herbert. *36 Children.* New York: The New American Library, 1967.

———. "Writing Their Way to Self-Acceptance." *Grade Teacher* 87 (1969):8-10.

Lamoreaux, Lillian A., and Lee, Dorris May. *Learning to Read Through Experience.* New York: Appleton-Century-Crofts, 1943.

Lee, Dorris May, and Allen, R. V. *Learning to Read Through Experience.* New York: Appleton-Century-Crofts, 1963.

Lowenfeld, Viktor, and Brittain, W. Lambert. *Creative and Mental Growth,* 4th ed. New York: The Macmillan Co., 1964.

Milner, Esther. "A Study of the Relationship Between Reading Readiness in Grade One School Children and Patterns of Parent-Child Interaction." *Child Development* 22 (1951):95-112.

National Council of Teachers of English. *The English Language Arts.* New York: Appleton-Century-Crofts, 1952.

Petty, Walter T., and Bowen, Mary E. *Slithery Snakes and Other Aids to Children's Writing.* New York: Appleton-Century-Crofts, 1967.

Smith, Henry P., and Dechant, Emerald V. *Psychology in Teaching Reading.* Englewood Cliffs, N. J.: Prentice-Hall, Inc., 1961.

Stauffer, Russell G. *The Language Experience Approach to the Teaching of Reading.* New York: Harper & Row, Publishers, 1970.

Strickland, Ruth G. *The Language Arts in the Elementary School.* New York: D. C. Heath and Co., 1963.

Trauger, Wilma K. *Language Arts in Elementary Schools.* New York: McGraw-Hill Co., 1963.

5

"Every Young Child Is an Artist": Books that Lead to Art Experiences

Art expression as an extension of oral language and writing is a very effective means by which a child can communicate his feelings and ideas to others and, at the same time, experience the profound sense of release that accompanies creative effort. As Nancy Larrick writes, "Creative activities turn dormant buds into blossoms. Any child or adult expands as he realizes that he is expressing himself in his own way. His attitudes and behavior are influenced by his new sense of individuality."[1]

An art program designed for young children should have as its basic purpose the eliciting of free expression from those children. Each activity and experience should be seen as a means of releasing the creative urge in wholesome and childlike ways. By nature, all young children have such a creative urge. They are imaginative, inventive, eager, and original until they have lived long enough to learn clichés and stereotypes that stifle the

1. Nancy Larrick, *A Teacher's Guide to Children's Books* (Columbus, Ohio: Charles E. Merrill Publishers, 1963), p. 147.

creative impulse. This reality of "diminishing creativity" makes the art curriculum for young children all the more important.

> . . . all humans have some creative potential whose release produces a measure of satisfaction. Therefore, a curriculum designed to encourage creativeness holds value for all students, not merely the creatively gifted minority.[2]

Modern education is at last directing its attention toward providing creative opportunity in every area of education, pre-school through college. Research findings have brought about this emphasis by making known the importance of the creative personality to our society. Burton and Heffernan write in the introduction to their handbook on creativity:

> The development of personality is desirable in and for itself. Meanings, attitudes, and appreciations are distinctly enhanced through efforts at creative expression. Creative self-expression is a normal characteristic of desirable living. The person whose response is original, inventive, and atypical is extremely important socially, because progress takes place through constructive variations from the accepted, the conventional, and the routine.[3]

Because the expression or the process itself is more important to young children than the finished product, teachers must not let themselves become unduly concerned with the *results* of a child's efforts in art. A young child expresses what he *feels* about things, which may mean large splotches of color applied in a purely abstract arrangement. This kind of painting is, of course, a more honest and sincere form of expression than he will be able to duplicate later on. For this reason, it should be appreciated, enjoyed and encouraged by adults who are significant to the child.

For teachers who are interested in promoting creativity in young children, Wilson and Robeck developed three basic themes to guide them. Those themes are: that creativity, like intelligence, exists to some degree in all people; that creative behavior is learned and therefore can be taught; and that children's creativity is built on the mental, aesthetic, and emotional patterns that have accumulated.[4]

When art for young children is viewed as a means of self-expression and also as a mode of communication with others, it becomes a perfect corollary to literature. Through many happy experiences with artistic,

2. John Curtis Gowan, George D. Demos, and E. Paul Torrance, *Creativity: Its Educational Implications* (New York: John Wiley & Sons, Inc., 1967), p. 205.
3. William H. Burton and Helen Heffernan, *The Step Beyond: Creativity* (Washington, D. C.: National Education Association, 1964), p. 1.
4. John A. R. Wilson and Mildred C. Robeck, "Creativity in the Very Young," *Teaching for Creative Endeavor*, ed. William B. Michael (Bloomington: Indiana University Press, 1968), pp. 55-56.

well-written children's books, young children grow to feel that beauty and color are important to their lives and that books are ever-present sources of information, inspiration, and aesthetic satisfaction.

Creative art-literature experiences occur in the classroom when boys and girls are moved by a good story well told or read, when art materials are made available, and when time and space are allowed for experimentation with the materials. On the other hand, true creativity is seldom expressed when each story is followed by the "en masse" assignment, "Use crayons to make a nice picture of your favorite part."

Most teachers of young children would agree that two keys to a successful art program for preschool and primary children are self-selection of art activities and freedom of expression. However, with increasing facility and maturity in the use of art materials, children can profit from planned art activities initiated and supervised by the teacher. Freedom of choice and expression need not be thwarted. Books make a natural springboard for such planned activities.

On the following pages are presented some art activities that have proven successful and appropriate for young children. Suggestions are also made for books that are well-suited to introduce, accompany, or culminate the various art projects described. It cannot be overemphasized that many children will not be ready for a structured art activity. Those children should be encouraged to pursue individual interests until such time as they choose to take part in the more directed art activities.

Mural Making

Murals, or wall paintings, go back to the time when prehistoric man scratched pictures in outline on the rock walls of his cave. His drawings offer evidence that man has always been moved to creative endeavor by strong artistic impulses and that group effort was and is a pleasant way to work. Mural making remains one of the most rewarding group activities for children of all ages.

The most popular medium for mural making in the elementary classroom is tempera paint applied with large soft brushes. Ordinarily, a long strip of white wrapping paper or shelf paper is spread on the floor of the classroom or hall and small groups of children gather around it to paint. Later the mural is attached to the wall for display.

The children will be much more pleased with the finished mural if they have planned sufficiently in advance and have an idea of what the overall composition will be like. If films, slides, or prints are available, they will enjoy seeing some of the great murals that have been used to adorn buildings in various parts of the world. It should be emphasized before the children begin painting that shapes and forms on a mural must be large, bold, and with a minimum of small detail.

Opportunities for using literature in mural composition are almost limitless if children are encouraged to interpret favorite stories and poems in their own way. Books that help to create strong mental images of the beauty in nature are excellent raw material for group paintings of the

Fig. 5.1. Detail of a mural painted by parents at a P.T.A. meeting after hearing a reading of *White Snow, Bright Snow,* by Alvin Tresselt and Roger Duvoisin.

mural type. Such books might include: *A Tree Is Nice, The Little Island, The Little House, The Happy Owls, Time of Wonder, The Big Snow,* and *Switch on the Night.*

Frieze Construction

A frieze is a long, narrow, horizontal band or border used for decorative purposes. In Greek architecture, the frieze was richly carved with hundreds of figures of people, plants, and animals. This band of low-relief architectural sculpture was usually located at the top of the outer wall of ancient temples.

In today's classroom, the frieze consists of a long, narrow band of paper on which numerous objects and figures made by children have been pasted. Frieze making is unsurpassed as a group activity for young children. It provides practice in sketching, painting, cutting, and pasting.

Fig. 5.2. Detail of a frieze made by seven-year-olds after hearing Eugene Field's poem, "The Duel." Large pages were first filled with crayon gingham and calico designs. The dogs and cats were then cut from the pages, arranged in pairs and pasted on the border.

Above all, the children are given the satisfaction of creating something of beauty. When all the children have made original contributions to the frieze, it is always lovely to look at.

Any good tale of the accumulative type in which animals, objects, or events increase one after the other up to the climax offers an excellent entrée to the planning of a frieze. Children can then be given the privilege of making as many additions to the border as time and inclination will allow. Some books that have been used by teachers to initiate a frieze project are: *Millions of Cats, Caps for Sale, Mr. Popper's Penguins, A Sky Full of Dragons, The 500 Hats of Bartholomew Cubbins,* and *Alligators All Around.*

Fig. 5.3. Every cat on this frieze made by six-year-olds has a distinct personality; no two are alike.

Collage

"Collage" comes from the French word "coller" which means to glue or paste something in place. Thus, a collage is made by pasting different textures and shapes of material to a flat surface such as paper, wood or cardboard to form an interesting and pleasing arrangement.

Collage materials may include fabrics and papers of varying textures and colors, soft wire, ribbon, buttons, yarn, seeds, macaroni, small toys and boxes, excelsior, toothpicks, straws, cotton, wood shavings, and countless other materials that are interesting in pattern, texture, color, or shape.

Materials for collage should be collected over a period of time by the teacher and students until an ample supply is available. The materials may then be sorted and filed in shoe boxes with the ends labeled as to contents. For children who cannot yet read, small scraps of the material may be glued on the boxes instead of labels to identify the contents.

The collage technique is especially good for those children who think that art must always be realistic representation. Collage lends itself to abstract and semi-abstract design. Storybook characters and scenes make fine subjects for collage projects. Such work should flow naturally from the child's imagination and interests without undue influence from book illustrations or teacher suggestions.

Fanciful animal stories in which the animal characters act like people, and often like small children, afford popular subject matter for collage construction. Such books might include: *Rabbit Hill, The Story of Ferdinand, Charlotte's Web, The Story of Babar, The Story of Ping, Make Way for Ducklings, Angus and the Ducks, and Theodore Turtle.*

Fig. 5.4. This is an eight-year-old boy's imaginative version of "Dividing Night" from *Rabbit Hill.* All materials for the collage came from a classroom scrap box, with the exception of the carrot seed package which he brought from home.

Mosaic

It has been said that Mesopotamian builders as early as the third millenium B.C. used small stones to cover the surface of their wood for color and protection. Mosaic is used in exactly the same way today, to cover a surface with small pieces of material in order to form an entirely new covering that is more attractive and durable than the original.

Each small piece of material used in a mosaic is called a "tessera," which is Latin for square piece; the plural is "tesserae." Tesserae may be composed of cut paper, cardboard, egg shells, pebbles, tile, seeds, linoleum, or bits of wood. The design for the mosaic is drawn on heavy cardboard or thin wood and each tessera is glued to the surface one at a time until all the areas have been filled in.

Mosaics are fun to do and are easy enough for young children. The finished product almost always turns out to be a handsome work of art whether made by an individual or by a group of children.

Students enjoy selecting a favorite book character to be captured in mosaic form. Using a crayon or felt point pen, the children sketch the shape of a storybook character in bold outline directly on the surface to be covered. The shape is filled in with glued tesserae and the background

Fig. 5.5. Pete Rabbit was chosen as their favorite storybook character, and was depicted in mosaic form by a group of six-year-olds. Tesserae were pieces cut from color ads in old magazines. The original shape was sketched by a committee of children using a black crayon on large white wrapping paper.

is added last. The finished mosaic is then ready to be trimmed and matted for display.

Books that have strong central characters that may be easily depicted by children and therefore suitable for mosaic are: *The Tale of Peter Rabbit, The Gingerbread Boy, Petunia, Veronica, Swimmy, and Johnny Crow's Garden.*

Montage

"Montage" comes from the French word "monter" which means "to mount." A montage is a composite picture made by combining several pictures or photographs to create a new photographic image.

In the elementary classroom, a student creates a montage by cutting pictures from magazines and pasting them together (mounting them) on a surface with edges slightly overlapping, to illustrate an association of ideas. For example, if the student wished to illustrate the concept "red," he might use an advertisement of a bottle of catsup, a red car, a red dress, a glass of tomato juice, or any other picture that is basically red. He then pastes them together to create a totally new image that says "red" with much greater impact than any single picture could convey.

The montage technique is not only enjoyable as an art process, but has the advantage of giving young children needed practice in eye-hand-mind coordination as they select, classify, cut, arrange, and paste. The finished montage will have meaning for all who view it if it is labeled appropriately with the idea or feeling it is intended to convey.

Some books that have been used successfully to inspire the montage process are: *Hailstones and Halibut Bones* (montage of colors), *The Little Auto* (montage of cars), *Mr. Rabbit and the Lovely Present* (montage of fruit), *Peter's Chair* (montage of furniture), *A Baby Sister for Frances* (montage of babies), and *Daddies, What They Do All Day* (montage of men at work).

Easel Painting

Probably the single most significant art activity for young children is painting with tempera paint at an art easel. Every day, throughout the entire school day, the easel should stand ready and waiting for children to use when they feel the urge to create a picture with paint.

An ample supply of newsprint paper, cut to fit the size of the easel, should be made available. A large twelve-inch brush is needed for each color of tempera paint being used so that colors may stay bright and clear.

The paint must be thick enough so that the brush can carry a full load of paint. A man's discarded shirt makes a fine artist's smock, and a low line with clothespins is a necessity for drying the large paintings.

Many times children will wish simply to experiment with bold splashes of color, but just as often they will want to paint a specific picture. Again, literature can provide the needed input for something to talk about, write about, and paint.

Folk literature of all types is unsurpassed as a catalyst for creative activity. Elements of folk tales, myths, legends, and fables consistently appear in the spontaneous writing and painting of children. Adults who work with children should not fail to share their knowledge of folk literature with the children, and every experience with literature of this type needs to be accompanied by opportunities for the children to give personal expression to the story. Easel painting is always a ready outlet for such expression.

The following books are examples of the abundant wealth of riches available in the area of folk literature: *The Three Billy Goats Gruff*, *Cinderella*, *The Legend of the Willow Plate*, *Aesop's Fables*, and *A Book of Myths*.

Fig. 5.6. Babe, the Blue Ox as perceived by a third-grade boy. It was painted in tempera during a study of tall tales. The class had conducted a debate on the distance between Babe's horns, and the boy included the crow that was caught in a blizzard while trying to fly from one horn to the other.

Studying the Art in Children's Books

Many of the great artists from all over the world have found in children's books a fertile field for their talents. They know children to be severe critics with a sure eye for banality, but also very receptive, appreciative and completely honest in their appraisal. An audience of such perception is bound to stimulate an illustrator to his best effort. Such excellence has given today's children an unparalleled selection of artistic, well-written books from which to choose.

Not only are the best books entertaining and beautiful to look at, but they also offer an endless array of art media and processes for the child's consideration. The home or classroom that owns even a modest collection of fine picture books has a veritable art gallery at its disposal.

Unfortunately, with increased facility in printing and in art reproduction techniques, an outpouring of valueless books for children have been marketed. Every day it becomes more imperative that teachers, parents, and children find ways to ferret out the treasures that do exist in literature. With fewer quiet hours available for reading, and with funds for books at a premium, it seems a tragedy to waste either on books that have no lasting value.

Probably the best way to gain skill in recognizing quality in children's books is to make a thorough study of some of the finest that have been published and use those as a measuring stick to judge others. The Caldecott Award books are examples of excellence.

The Caldecott Medal

In order to pay tribute to the artists who spend their time creating outstanding illustrations for children's books, the American Library Association established a special award in 1937. The award was named for Randolph Caldecott, an English illustrator of children's books during the nineteenth century. It is said that his illustrations point him out as the first artist to illustrate books from a child's point of view. When the sculptor René Paul Chambellan (famous for his sculpture in Rockefeller Center) was commissioned to design the medal, he turned to Caldecott's own work for inspiration, and chose two of his drawings to be reproduced on the medal itself.

The Caldecott Award is presented each year to "the artist of the most distinguished American picture book for children." The selection of the winner is made by a committee of the Children's Services Division of the American Library Association. A replica of the medal is attached to the book jacket of winning books for easy identification in bookstores and libraries. (A complete list of the Caldecott medal books, their illustrators and publishers, is given in Appendix A.)

The first Caldecott Award was presented to Dorothy P. Lathrop in 1938 for her distinguished picture book *Animals of the Bible.* Since that time the medal has been awarded annually to an American illustrator for a book published the preceding year. Two author-artists have won the award twice. Robert McCloskey won the medal in 1942 for *Make Way for Ducklings* and in 1958 for *Time of Wonder*. Marcia Brown won the medal in 1955 for *Cinderella* and in 1962 for *Once a Mouse*.

Fig. 5.7. This double-page illustration from Marcia Brown's book, *How Hippo!* holds fascination for preschool children, perhaps because it shows so well the magic of communication between mother and child. (Illustration reproduced with permission of Charles Scribner's Sons from *How Hippo!* by Marcia Brown. Copyright © 1969 Marcia Brown.)

Young children are curious about the Caldecott Award, and often request information about the author and illustrator of winning books. They seem to find fascination in a book that has won an important award for its art work. Additionally, an unusual feature of the Caldecott Award books is their appeal to all ages. Such attraction makes them excellent material for cross-age grouping. Older children read them aloud to younger children and, in the process, polish and refine their own reading skills.

Most of the Caldecott books remain popular with children, perhaps because they have been presented in a variety of ways by adults who like them. Children have always been drawn to great books when parents have read them aloud at home, when teachers have presented them in class for reading and discussion, and when librarians have found interesting ways to display them.

Significant adults in a child's life are responsible for providing him with a rich program of art and literature. Incidental exposure to a few moth-eaten library books will never meet the aesthetic needs of a child.

CHILDREN'S BOOKS FOR ART EXPERIENCES

Aesop's Fables, illustrated by Alice and Martin Provenson. New York: The Golden Press, 1967. Forty of the favorite tales of wise and foolish animals selected and adapted by a famous storyteller, Louis Untermeyer. The illustrations are humorous and clever, a perfect complement to the familiar old stories.

Alligators All Around, written and illustrated by Maurice Sendak. New York: Harper & Row, Publishers, 1962. A delightful nonsense alphabet book about alligators. A tiny book just right for small hands. Part of the Nutshell Library by Maurice Sendak.

Angus and the Ducks, written and illustrated by Marjorie Flack. Garden City, N. Y.: Doubleday & Co., Inc., 1930. Angus, a curious little Scotty dog, goes to investigate the quacking sound. The quacking turns to hissing and Angus quickly loses his curiosity—for three minutes at least.

A Baby Sister for Frances, written by Russell Hoban and illustrated by Lillian Hoban. New York: Harper & Row, Publishers, 1964. Watching her parents care for the new baby in the family, Frances feels alone and neglected until she finally decides to set things right by running away. Her parents understand her feelings and quickly take steps to make amends.

The Big Snow, written and illustrated by Berta and Elmer Hader. New York: The Macmillan Co., 1948. A realistic story of how various animals prepare themselves for winter, and of a kindly couple who puts out food for them when the big snow arrives. A good book to help make children sensitive to needs of wild animals.

A Book of Myths, illustrated by Helen Sewell. New York: The Macmillan Co., 1942. This is a selection of the most popular myths from Bulfinch's "Age of the Fable." It is a fine resource for storytelling in the middle grades. The line drawings are reminiscent of early Greek Art.

Caps for Sale, written and illustrated by Esphyr Slobodkina. New York: William R. Scott, Inc., 1947. A cap peddler who carries all his wares on his head is surprised to find they have been whisked away by a band of mischievous monkeys. How he finally persuades them to give back the caps is delightful fun for young children.

Charlotte's Web, written by E. B. White and illustrated by Garth Williams. New York: Harper & Row, Publishers, 1952. *Charlotte's Web* is a universally loved book of the modern talking beast tale variety. It is excellent for reading aloud, as a continued story, to eight-year-olds. Most children will then read the book for themselves—often more than once.

The 500 Hats of Bartholomew Cubbins, written and illustrated by Dr. Seuss (Theodore Geisel). New York: The Vanguard Press, 1938. The king orders Bartholomew to remove his plumed hat out of respect to His Majesty, and Bartholomew is quite willing to do so, but every time he removes it, another appears in its place. Each new hat is more elaborate than the one before, and the last is the most wonderful hat of all.

Hailstones and Halibut Bones, written by Mary O'Neill and illustrated by Leonard Weisgard. Garden City N. Y.: Doubleday & Co., 1961. Twelve poems by Mary O'Neill are used to describe the colors of the spectrum. By using familiar objects and images, she shows that each color has its own story to tell. The art work forms a perfect relationship with the poetry as each color is presented in picture form.

Johnny Crow's Garden, written and illustrated by Leslie Brooke. New York. Frederick Warne and Co., 1965. Johnny Crow stands out among the wise and foolish animals in the garden as having a unique personality. The book has been very popular with young children since the first edition was issued in 1903.

The Legend of the Willow Plate, written by Alvin Tresselt and Nancy Cleaver, and illustrated by Joseph Low. New York: Parents' Magazine Press, 1968. Practically everyone has seen the blue willow design on dinnerware, but not all people know the ancient Chinese legend that it portrays. This book offers a sensitive, poetic retelling of the old story.

The Little Auto, written and illustrated by Lois Lenski. New York: Henry Z. Walck, Inc., 1940. Mr. Small drives the little auto exactly like a young child would like to do with all the familiar gestures and movements. A simple story without plot, but one young children request again and again. Other books in the series are *The Little Train, The Little Airplane,* and *The Little Fire Engine.*

The Little House, written and illustrated by Virginia Lee Burton. Boston: Houghton Mifflin Co., 1942. A little country house is engulfed as the city gradually builds around it. The story shows some of the undesirable aspects of technological and industrial progress. Includes a lovely description of the four seasons as observed by the little house.

Make Way for Ducklings, written and illustrated by Robert McCloskey. New York: The Viking Press, 1941. After Mr. and Mrs. Mallard have hatched out a fine family of eight ducklings, they must teach the little ones to swim, dive, walk in a line, to come when called, and to keep a safe distance from things with wheels.

Mr. Popper's Penguins, written by Richard and Florence Atwater and illustrated by Robert Lawson. Boston: Little, Brown & Co., 1938. When he is not working at his job of house painting, Mr. Popper reads books on polar exploration. His life is changed completely when Admiral Drake sends him a penguin from the Antarctic which he names Captain Cook. An aquarium sends Mr. Popper a mate for Captain Cook and soon there are ten more penguins in the house!

Petunia, written and illustrated by Roger Duvoisin. New York: Alfred A. Knopf, Inc., 1950. Petunia, a humorous, lovable goose, is more like a person than a barnyard fowl. She is a wise philosopher and a unique individual. Other books in the series are *Petunia and the Song* and *Petunia Takes a Trip.*

Rabbit Hill, written and illustrated by Robert Lawson. New York: The Viking Press, 1944. A modern talking beast tale that is extremely popular with children in the middle grades. It teaches a reverance for all of nature's small creatures, from rabbits to field mice.

A Sky Full of Dragons, written by Mildred Whatley Wright and illustrated by Carroll Dolezal. Austin Tex.: Steck-Vaughn Co., 1969. The story of how a Chinese boy named Lee Chow and his grandfather use rice paper and paint to make a sky full of dragon kites for Lee Chow's friends. What Lee Chow is given in return is something he wants more than anything. Beautifully illustrated.

The Story About Ping, written by Marjorie Flack and illustrated by Kurt Wiese. New York: The Viking Press, 1933. The adventures of a small duck who lives with his brothers, sisters, cousins, aunts, and uncles on a Chinese junk in the Yangtze River. Authentic Chinese legendry and background.

The Story of Babar, written and illustrated by Laurent de Brunhoff. New York: Random House, 1937. Translated from French for American children, Babar's adventures have been popular here for many years. Babar is an elephant who dresses in a business suit and acts very much like a man. This is the first of a dozen books about Babar and his friends.

Swimmy, written and illustrated by Leo Leonni. New York: Pantheon Books, Inc., 1963. Swimmy, a frightened and lonely little black fish, explores the depths of the ocean to find a family he can adopt. When he finds a family of fish with whom he can swim, he uses his intelligence and creativity to teach his new brothers and sisters a way to protect themselves from larger fish. Lovely illustrations by a famous artist.

Switch on the Night, written by Ray Bradbury and illustrated by Madeleine Gekiere. New York: Pantheon Books, Inc., 1955. The story of a little boy who does not like the night. He is lonely and unhappy while the other children run and play in the dark. Finally, a little girl teaches him how to switch on the night with a light switch. He finds that in switching on the night he can switch on crickets, frogs, stars, and a great white moon.

The Tale of Peter Rabbit, written and illustrated by Beatrix Potter. New York: Frederick Warne & Co., Inc., 1901. One of the most perfect stories for early childhood. Young children see themselves in Peter as he disobeys, finds himself in serious trouble, repents, is punished, and is finally accepted and forgiven.

The Three Billy Goats Gruff, illustrated by Marcia Brown. New York: Harcourt Brace Jovanovich, Inc., 1957. One of the finest versions available of a folk tale that has been a favorite of children for generations. Illustrated by one of the most versatile of all artists for children.

Time of Wonder, written and illustrated by Robert McCloskey. New York: The Viking Press, 1957. This beautiful book of water color paintings tells the story of life on a Maine island before and after a hurricane. Children go about exploring the seashore and the forests beyond just as children have always done. An excellent account is given of the way parents protect children during a crisis.

A Tree Is Nice, written by Janice May Udry and illustrated by Marc Simont. New York: Harper & Row, Publishers, 1956. The text and pictures are combined to show every child who reads or looks at the book the joys and delights a nice tree has to offer. The book not only gives childlike directions for planting a tree, but describes the pride that comes in watching it thrive and grow.

Veronica, written and illustrated by Roger Duvoisin. New York: Alfred A. Knopf, Inc., 1961. A hippopotamus named Veronica wants to become famous and conspicuous. She becomes very conspicuous by leaving the herd and walking boldly down the main street of a pink and white city. Trouble brews as Veronica becomes *too* conspicuous.

BIBLIOGRAPHY

Aller, Doris, and Aller, Diane. *Mosaics.* Menlo Park, Calif.: Lane Book Co., 1959.

Burton, William H., and Heffernan, Helen. *The Step Beyond: Creativity.* Washington, D. C.: National Education Association, 1964.

Carlson, Ruth Kearney. *Literature for Children: Enrichment Ideas.* Dubuque, Iowa: Wm. C. Brown Co., Publishers, 1970.

Eisner, Elliot W., and Ecker, David W. *Readings in Art Education.* Waltham, Mass.: Blaisdell Publishing Co., 1966.

Gaitskell, Charles D., and Hurwitz, Al. *Children and Their Art.* New York: Harcourt Brace Jovanovich, Inc., 1970.

Gowan, John Curtis; Demos, George D.; Torrence, E. Paul. *Creativity: Its Educational Implications.* New York: John Wiley & Sons, Inc., 1967.

Larrick, Nancy. *A Teacher's Guide to Children's Books.* Columbus, Ohio: Charles E. Merrill, Books, Inc., 1963.

Lord, Lois. *Collage and Construction.* New York: Scholastic Book Services, 1958.

Lowenfeld, Viktor, and Brittain, W. Lambert. *Creative and Mental Growth.* 4th ed. New York: The Macmillan Co., 1964.

Smith, Irene. *A History of the Newbery and Caldecott Medals.* New York: The Viking Press, 1957.

Wilson, John A. R., and Robeck, Mildred C. "Creativity in the Very Young." *Teaching for Creative Endeavor.* Edited by William B. Michael. Bloomington: Indiana University Press, 1968.

6

"Better Homes and Kindergartens Cookbook": Books that Lead to Cooking Experiences

Of all the learning experiences a teacher might plan for young children, none is more versatile than preparing food in the classroom. Children are fascinated by cooking and eating, and yet, it has been found that they know very little about the origin, preservation, and preparation of the food they eat every day. The fact that children do have strong feelings about food and actually understand so little about it makes cooking a very important area for teaching.

A reliable way to make each cooking experience a cohesive learning unit with interrelated steps is to have it spring naturally from an excellent piece of children's literature. Since authors are aware of children's interest in food, many good books have been written in which food and the acquiring of food is the main theme. As a matter of fact, storytellers were creating and telling tales about food long before such stories were recorded in print. The old folk tales abound with the problems of earning bread and of imaginary tables laden with rich and exotic foods. Such stories are extremely popular with modern children.

Reading aloud and discussing a good book in which food is an important element is usually all the motivation necessary to begin planning a

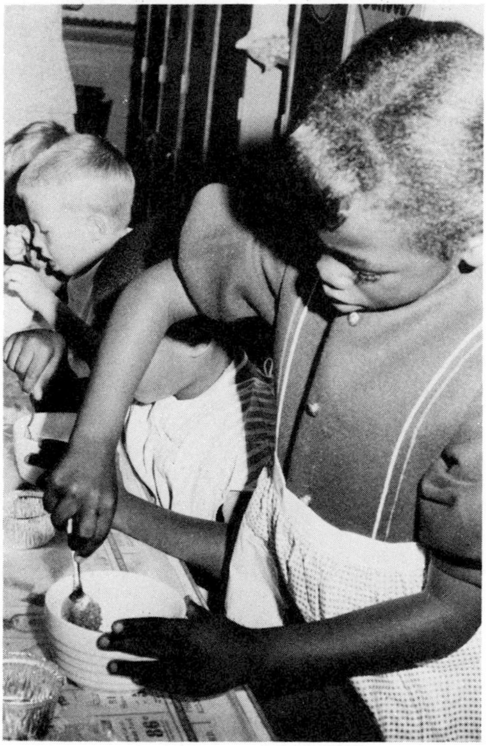

Fig. 6.1. Some children can hardly wait to sample the finished product while others are satisfied with the cooking activity itself. (Courtesy of Anahuac Independent School District, Anahuac, Texas.)

cooking activity with young children. Cooking makes the book memorable, and, in turn, the story serves to make cooking in the classroom even more important.

If the cooking activities are appropriate to the developmental level of children and if they are introduced at an opportune time, all areas of the curriculum are enriched and enhanced in the process. Skills in language arts are acquired as children become involved with the exciting vocabulary of food. They learn sequential order in a natural way as they follow a recipe on the tape recorder or on a recipe chart made of rebus drawings.

Social studies concepts are gained as the children plan, organize, and cooperate to carry out the cooking tasks. They learn to set a table, to take part in appropriate conversation at the table, and to assume responsibility for cleaning up. They begin to understand that mealtime is a great socializing practice and is much more in our lives than the fulfillment of a creature comfort.

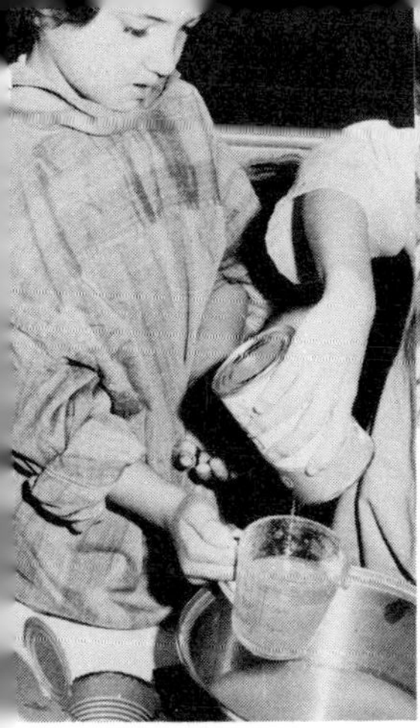
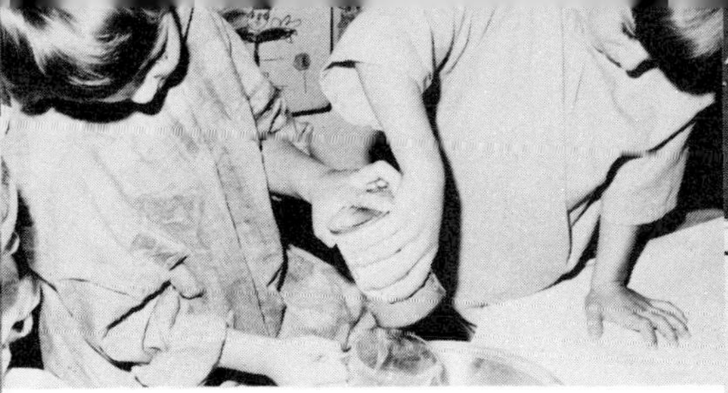
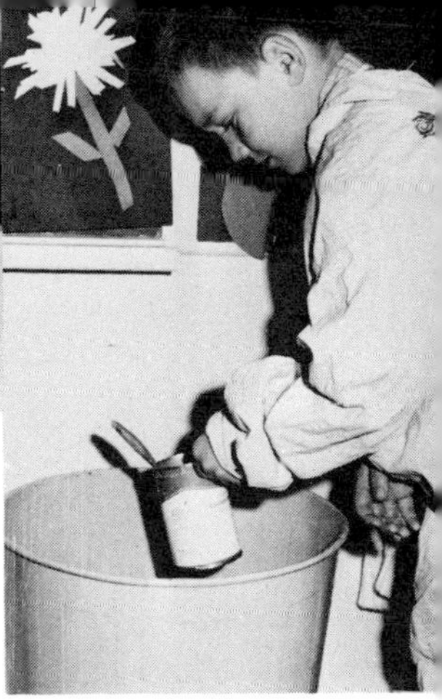

Figs. 6.2, 6.3, and 6.4. Cooperation in the cooking task brings social satisfaction. Two youngsters measure the broth which shows graphic proof that there are two cups in each can. Another student shares the clean-up tasks. (Courtesy of South Park Independent School District, Beaumont, Texas.)

Cooking experiences are rich in science and mathematics learnings. The children count, measure, estimate, add, subtract, multiply, divide and learn about fractions. They observe and discuss the chemical reactions as ingredients are mixed together. They watch the changes in form that foods take when heated and cooled. They are able to examine gelatin as a powder, as a liquid, and as a solid. Voilà! Chemistry in the kindergarten!

Food preparation is an excellent vehicle for teaching health and safety. Teaching nutrition to young children has always been difficult and changing undesirable attitudes about food is an important objective in kindergarten cooking. Some children are poorly nourished simply because they refuse to try new foods, and variety in their diet is totally lacking. However, we know that they usually do eat, and with relish, what they have prepared—even vegetables!

All the necessary safety precautions should be emphasized where food preparation is in progress. Children can be taught to clean up spills promptly, to handle utensils correctly and to follow safety rules to the letter. They can learn proper respect for any food that is hot. Cooking should always be carefully supervised by the teacher. In addition, an aide, a student teacher, or other interested adults may be asked to help supervise the cooking activities. The table range or hot plate should be placed at the child's eye level. Such precautions pay dividends in accident prevention and subsequent learnings may carry over into life outside the classroom.

Learning theory tells us that young children prefer interesting work over entertainment or other activities. Cooking is interesting work. Some teachers have always believed that children and cooking go together. Others feel that children and cooking and literature go together—a recipe for fun and learning.

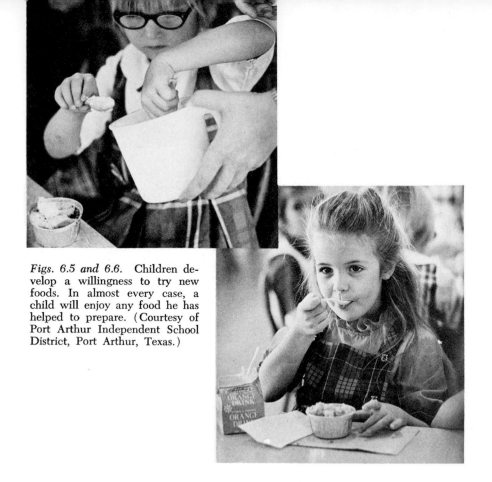

Figs. 6.5 and 6.6. Children develop a willingness to try new foods. In almost every case, a child will enjoy any food he has helped to prepare. (Courtesy of Port Arthur Independent School District, Port Arthur, Texas.)

Hints to the Teacher

All cooking activities must be closely supervised and most teachers will want another adult present to help work with groups and with individual children. The helper might be a student teacher, an aide, an interested parent, or a cook from the school cafeteria. The teacher should review the procedures in advance so that the helper will be able to offer the right assistance and will not take over tasks that children should do for themselves.

Since so few classrooms are equipped with cook stoves, it is usually necessary to improvise. A table range, an electric fry pan, or a hot plate will usually suffice. Such small appliances offer an added advantage of being at the child's eye level. Other alternatives include the stove in the school cafeteria or the oven of a cooperative parent who lives near the school.

It is best to begin with simple cooking activities in which good results will be more or less guaranteed. The children are then ready to proceed to more complex recipes and to more detailed units of work.

It is well to try each recipe before presenting it to the children. At such time the teacher might work out a sequence of steps for each group of students and write them in a plan book for ready reference. A check-off list of needed materials and ingredients is always helpful.

Adults should recognize that the importance of cooking in the classroom lies in the doing and not necessarily in the finished product. In most cases, the cooking will provide a small snack for the children, and not a full meal.

If expense is a problem, the food prepared in the classroom may be used as part of the mid-morning snack and paid for out of the funds provided. Many schools will allow teachers to requisition foods if they are used as instructional material. Some foods, such as vegetables for soup, may be brought by children from home.

The Poppy Seed Cakes

The Poppy Seed Cakes is a nonsensical book that is made up of a series of stories built around the misadventures of a small boy named Andrewshek. It is easy for young children to identify with Andrewshek as he finds himself involved in one mishap after another. Each time he repents and promises to do better, but finds it utterly impossible to stay out of mischief. These warm and human stories are excellent for reading aloud and perfect for storytelling. Auntie Katushka's good poppy seed cakes are referred to throughout the book and one story actually lists the ingredients:

> One lovely Saturday morning Andrewshek's Auntie Katushka took some butter and some sugar and some flour and some milk and seven eggs and she rolled out some nice little cakes. Then she sprinkled each cake with some of the poppy seeds which she had brought from the old country.[1]

Recipe for Poppy Seed Cakes

1 cup butter or margine	2 cups flour
1/2 cup sugar	poppy seeds

1. Margery Clark, *The Poppy Seed Cakes* (Garden City, N. Y.: Doubleday & Co., Inc., 1924).

Blend butter, sugar and flour with fingers. Roll into small balls the size of a walnut. (Let each child work on a small piece of waxed paper sprinkled with flour.) Flatten each ball slightly with a floured spoon. Sprinkle cakes with poppy seeds. Bake in a slow oven, about 300°, until lightly brown around the edges. Cool and serve with a beverage at snack-time.

Related Activities

Language Arts

Tell or read aloud a story from *The Poppy Seed Cakes* each day until the series is completed.

Lead a discussion about Andrewshek's experiences and about his relationship with the kindly Auntie Katushka.

Make paper models of the butter, sugar, flour, milk, eggs, and poppy seeds for children to arrange on the felt board in sequential order as they appear in Auntie Katushka's recipe. Compare Auntie Katushka's recipe with the simpler one.

Social Science

Study the illustrations by Maud and Miska Petersham and discuss the clothing worn by Andrewshek, Auntie Katushka, and Erminka.

Talk about the wonderous and rhythmic names of the characters. How are they different from names we hear every day?

Disscuss ways in which children everywhere are alike.

Plan a tea party like Auntie Katushka's and serve the freshly baked poppy seed cakes.

Science and Mathematics

Measure ingredients. Study the markings on the measuring cups.

Count the cookies together and decide how to divide them evenly among the class.

Study the thermostat on the oven and set it at 300°.

Let children estimate the number of minutes it will take to brown the cakes. Watch the clock and count the minutes it actually takes to bake them.

Health and Safety

Emphasize the importance of cleanliness in handling food.

Supervise thorough washing of hands with soap before dough is kneaded.

Elect committees of children to wash the mixing bowl, measuring cup, and cookie sheets.

Art

Study the decorative designs that ornament the pages of *The Poppy Seed Cakes.*

Show children how to make similar designs. Have them repeat a simple flower drawing on a sheet of art paper that has been folded four times. When the paper is unfolded, there will be sixteen squares in which to repeat the chosen pattern. Display the designs as a border around the bulletin board.

Prepare a frieze showing the ducks that spoiled Erminka's red boots. Let each child draw, color, and cut out several ducks to paste on a large blue "pond" that the teacher has previously mounted on the bulletin board.

Blueberries for Sal

Little Sal and her mother go up one side of Blueberry Hill to pick blueberries for the winter while Little Bear and his mother come up the other side of Blueberry Hill to eat blueberries for the winter. Somehow Little Sal gets lost and follows Little Bear's mother; at the same time Little Bear gets lost and follows Little Sal's mother. The two mothers are properly astonished when they discover the mistake. Little Sal and Little Bear take the mix-up in stride and all ends well.[2]

The exact parallelism in the story and also in the illustrations makes an excellent book for reading and discussion in kindergarten. Robert McCloskey uses a beautiful blue ink, the color of blueberries, for the very realistic illustrations.

Recipe for Blueberry Cupcakes

1 package frozen blueberries
1 package blueberry muffin mix

Mix cupcakes according to directions on the blueberry muffin package. Pour batter into foil disposable muffin cups. Fill each only one-half full. Bake cupcakes in the classroom by using an electric fry pan. Place muffin cups on a wire rack in the fry pan and cover the pan while baking.

2. Robert McCloskey, *Blueberries for Sal* (New York: The Viking Press, 1948).

Thaw frozen blueberries while cupcakes are baking. While the muffins are still warm, spoon some of the blueberries on each one for a delicious and colorful topping. Serve with milk at snack time.

Related Activities

Language Arts

Read *Blueberries for Sal* to the class and give the children an opportunity to study and discuss the illustrations.

Encourage the children to retell the story. Keep it moving by asking, "What happened next? And then what happened?"

By using the "fruits" page in a picture dictionary, compare blueberries with other berries.

Make a chart of berries by cutting pictures from old seed catalogues and from labels on cans of berries.

Make a list of new words used in the blueberry unit and review them with the children.

Social Science

Locate Maine on a large map of the United States. Discuss the fact that Robert McCloskey lived there and that blueberries grew near his home.

Collect travel folders and pictures of Maine.

Discuss the protective love that mothers feel for their young.

Read aloud *One Morning in Maine.*[3] Compare it with *Blueberries for Sal.*

Science and Mathematics

Compare the way in which Sal and her mother stored berries for the winter with the way Little Bear and his mother stored berries for the winter. Develop the concept of animal hibernation.

Study the end pages of the book *Blueberries for Sal,* which show Sal and her mother canning blueberries in glass jars. Bring a glass jar used for canning to show the children. If possible, show a lid with a red rubber sealing ring like the one pictured.

If several sealing rings are available, let the children count them the way Sal is doing in the picture.

Compare freezing with canning as a way of preserving the blueberries.

Health and Safety

Use the electric fry pan or portable oven as an exhibit in a discussion of safety precautions to be observed while using electrical appliances.

3. Robert McCloskey, *One Morning in Maine* (New York: The Viking Press, 1952).

Involve the senses of sight, smell, and taste in sampling the blueberries. Develop a willingness to try new foods.

Art

Using crayons, decorate plain white paper napkins with a blueberry motif. With white paper towels, make matching place mats. Use the napkins and mats at snack time.

Chicken Soup with Rice

Chicken Soup with Rice, by Maurice Sendak, is composed of hilarious nonsense rhymes promoting chicken soup with rice every month of the year. At the end of the twelfth month, the story is summarized with the following rhyme:

I told you once
I told you twice
All seasons of the year
are nice
for eating chicken soup
with rice![4]

In addition to the paperback edition, the book is also available in minature form as part of the *Nutshell Library* by Maurice Sendak. Each one of the books in this set is 2 1/2 inches by 3 3/4 inches, just the right size for small hands. The four books are housed in a decorative slip case.

Recipe for Chicken Soup with Rice

8 cups seasoned chicken broth
1 cup chopped celery
1/2 cup rice

Heat the broth in a boiler. Add chopped celery and cook until tender. Add rice and cook until it is fluffy and tender. Cool and serve in paper cups with packaged toast or crackers.

Related Activities

Language Arts

Read *Chicken Soup with Rice* aloud several times until children are able to join in on the refrain.

Discuss events associated with each month of the year and show how the rhymes and illustrations depict each month.

4. Maurice Sendak, *Chicken Soup with Rice* (New York: Harper & Row, Publishers, 1962). Available in paperback from Scholastic Book Services, New York.

Compare illustrations in the paperback edition with the Nutshell Library version of *Chicken Soup with Rice.*

Social Science

Study the *Chicken Soup with Rice* calendar and repeat the names of the months in sequence.[5]

Talk about the meaning of "soup" and discuss soups that are popular in different parts of the country.

Science and Mathematics

Measure water in measuring cup.

Study the meaning of one-half cup.

Have children count out the needed number of paper cups.

Help children count out two crackers per person.

Examine grains of rice before and after heating. Show how they expand and soften when cooked.

Art

Let children look through old magazines for pictures of soups. They should be able to find cans, bowls, and cups of soup. Have them cut out the pictures and paste them on a large chart labeled "SOUP."

Health and Safety

Discuss the danger of boiling liquids. Show how the handle of a boiler should be turned toward the wall.

Wash hands before eating.

Emphasize the nutritional value of wholesome soup.

Bread and Jam for Frances

Frances is a young and very child-like badger who is unwilling to try any new food and insists on bread and jam three times a day. Her parents find a way to cure her of asking for bread and jam by serving her nothing else for a period of time. The Hobans have illustrated the book with soft charcoal drawings that give Frances and her family a delightful furry texture.

As Frances waits for the school bus, she sings:

Jam on biscuits, jam on toast,
Jam is the thing that I like most.
Jam is sticky, jam is sweet,

5. The *Chicken Soup with Rice* calendar is available from Scholastic Book Services, New York.

Jam is tasty, jam's a treat—
Raspberry, strawberry, gooseberry,
I'm very FOND . . . OF . . . JAM![6]

Recipe for Blackberry Jam

1 cup canned blackberries, drained
3/4 cup sugar
1 tablespoon Sure-Jell

Mix Sure-Jell with berries in sauce pan. Bring mixture to boil, stirring occasionally. Add sugar and boil one minute, stirring constantly. Cool and serve on slices of bread cut in half.

Related Activities

Language Arts

Read aloud the book *Bread and Jam for Frances.* Discuss the story. Why did Frances finally cry when given her favorite food, bread and jam?

Look at pictures of strawberries, gooseberries, blueberries, blackberries, and other berries. Discuss the differences in appearance.

Outline plans for making jam.

Write the recipe on a large chart. Read it to the children. Let them observe writing of chart. Show them how to follow a recipe in sequential order.

Social Science

Read aloud the other "Frances" books to show wholesome family relationships.

Explain how blackberries are a native American fruit, but were considered only a weed by early settlers.

Science and Mathematics

Show shape of bread before cutting it in half (square).

Examine shape of bread after cutting at an angle (triangle).

Show other examples of "one-half."

Measure ingredients in calibrated containers. Show markings.

Health and Safety

In discussing *Bread and Jam for Frances,* ask children to explain why parents want them to eat many kinds of food.

Talk about the taste of blackberry jam and show how the sampling of a new food can be an exciting adventure.

6. Russell and Lillian Hoban, *Bread and Jam for Frances* (New York: Harper & Row, Publishers, 1964). Available in paperback from Scholastic Book Services, New York.

Emphasize the importance of washing hands before eating finger foods.

Outline safety precautions to be observed when heating liquids.

Art

Using colored chalk, allow children to make large pieces of fruit on the want-ad sections of newspapers. Have children cut out the fruits and paste them (slightly overlapping the pieces) on a large chart to make a colorful collage. Label the chart, "Fruits We Like."

The Thanksgiving Story

The Thanksgiving Story, by Alice Dalgliesh, is a fictional account of the first Thanksgiving, beginning with the voyage of the Mayflower and ending with the first feast between the Pilgrims and the Indians.[7] Since the story is developed around the experiences of one family, it appeals to young children and brings the story closer to the present time.

The illustrations are colorful and authentic, a perfect complement to the traditional story. They include a cross-section diagram of the Mayflower.

This is a very good book to read aloud as a continued story, and it is also excellent for storytelling. The illustration of the Thanksgiving feast can be a springboard for many creative activities in the classroom, including the cooking of traditional foods.

Recipe for Individual Pumpkin Pies

The following ingredients will be needed for each child:

2 graham crackers
1 teaspoon sugar
1 tablespoon melted butter
1 small plastic bag
1 foil muffin cup

Let each child crush his two crackers in a small plastic bag. Add the sugar and melted butter and mix thoroughly. Have children press the crumb mixture into the muffin cup. The crust is then ready for filling.

The following recipe for filling should be prepared at home by the teacher and chilled overnight:

7. Alice Dalgliesh, *The Thanksgiving Story.* (New York: Charles Scribner's Sons, 1954).

Pumpkin Mallow Pie Filling

2 cans pumpkin	1 tsp. cinnamon
2 lbs. marshmallows	1 tsp. (scant) salt
2 cartons "Cool Whip"	

Cook mixture of pumpkin, marshallows, and spices over low heat until marshmallows melt. Cool. Chill two cartons of "Cool Whip" and beat until fluffy. Fold in pumpkin mixture. Take the filling to the classroom and allow each child to spoon some of the mixture into his pie shell. The pies may be topped with whipped cream or trimmed with chocolate chips. Cut recipe in half for a small class. Serve with milk at snack time.

Related Activities

Language Arts

Read aloud or tell *The Thanksgiving Story* and give children an opportunity to talk about their own understandings of the Thanksgiving holiday.

Prepare an exhibit of books and pictures about Thanksgiving. Encourage browsing.

Make a vocabulary chart of Thanksgiving words. Illustrate each one with a rebus drawing.

Compare a real pumpkin with a picture of a pumpkin and with the printed word "pumpkin."

Social Science

Plan and teach a simplified unit of the Thanksgiving holiday. Emphasize the meaning of the holiday.

Use a globe to trace the voyage of the Mayflower and a map to locate Plymouth.

In a dramatic play, act out *The Thanksgiving Story.*

Science and Mathematics

Measure ingredients for the pie crusts. Count out the graham crackers needed. Involve all the senses in making pie crusts.

Using the diagram in *The Thanksgiving Story,* study the parts of a ship.

Health and Safety

Discuss all the foods that were said to have been served at the first Thanksgiving dinner.

Art

Arrange a Thanksgiving centerpiece for the classroom.

Create a Thanksgiving collage by pasting pictures of foods cut from magazines on a large chart in the shape of a harvest table.

The Duchess Bakes a Cake

The Duchess Bakes A Cake is a book to be read aloud to children for pure fun. An impish duchess bakes a cake so light and fluffy that it lifts her up into the clouds. Gunhilde, the youngest of her thirteen daughters, suggests that they all begin eating the "light luscious delectable cake" to get her mother down. "How lovely!" the Duchess says. "Come let us sup. I'll start eating down; you start eating up."[8]

Flat poster-like folk art in brilliant colors is used to illustrate the hilarious story.

Recipe for One-Two-Three-Four Cake

1 cup shortening	3 cups sifted flour
2 cups sugar	3 teaspoons baking powder
1/4 teaspoon salt	1 cup milk
4 eggs, separated	1 teaspoon vanilla

Preheat oven to 375° F. Use two 9-inch round cake pans. Baking time is 35 to 40 minutes.

Cream shortening, sugar, and salt together until light and fluffy. Add beaten egg yolks and blend until smooth. Sift flour and baking powder together three times and add to first mixture with milk and vanilla. Fold in the stiffly beaten egg whites. Pour into greased and floured cake pans. Bake. Remove from pans immediately after baking. Cool on wire racks. At snack time, serve the cake while still warm with cups of cold milk.

Related Activities

Language Arts

Reread *The Duchess Bakes a Cake* during the waiting period while the cake bakes.

If the oven in the school lunch room is used for baking, compose a thank-you note to manager. The teacher can serve as recorder for the children's language.

Promote conversation at snack time.

8. Virginia Kahl, *The Duchess Bakes a Cake* (New York: Charles Scribner's Sons, 1955).

Social Science

Help children learn to take turns.

Teach cooperation and organization needed to carry out the complex task of baking a cake.

Practice setting the table.

Science and Mathematics

Add baking powder to water and observe chemical reaction.

Help children to hypothesize about what will happen to the batter as it bakes.

Measure the depth of the batter before baking. Record. Measure thickness of cake after baking. Compare the two figures.

Set oven timer. Synchronize with clock. Set alarm to go off when the cake is done.

Show the children how to test for doneness.

Health and Safety

Teach safety precautions regarding hot stove and hot pans. Demonstrate the use of insulated mittens. Caution: An adult should put the cake in the oven and also remove it.

Art

Make place mats by trimming edges of paper towels with crayon border. Slices of cake may be served directly on mats.

The Gingerbread Man

The rhythm of the language in this old folk tale has fascinated young children for ages. The gingerbread man repeats the same impertinent reply to all who try to stop him:

> Run, run
> As fast as you can.
> You can't catch me.
> I'm the gingerbread man.[9]

Each time he gains another pursuer, the gingerbread man adds one more line to his song until he is finally outwitted by the fox, and both the song and the gingerbread man come to an end. True to the folk tale style, the story ends abruptly and is tied up neatly with a flourish: "And that was the end of the gingerbread man!"

9. Ed Arno, *The Gingerbread Man* (New York: Scholastic Book Services, 1967).

Recipe for Gingerbread Men

4 cups sifted flour
1 tablespoon cinnamon
1 teaspoon salt
1 teaspoon baking powder
1 teaspoon ginger
1/2 cup shortening
1/2 cup firmly packed brown sugar
1 egg
1 cup molasses

Sift first five ingredients together and set aside. Cream shortening. Gradually add brown sugar, creaming until fluffy after each addition. Continue creaming while adding egg. Blend in molasses. Stir in dry ingredients. Chill dough overnight in the refrigerator.

Pinch off a ball of dough for each child who is working at the table. Let the children roll or pat dough to 1/4 inch thick on a lightly floured surface. (If they have a tendency to roll too much flour into the dough, powdered sugar may be substituted for flour.) Cut dough with gingerbread man cookie cutter or cut around cardboard pattern of a gingerbread man. A very good plan for making a more creative gingerbread man is to form a ball for the head, one for the body, and four smaller ones for the arms and legs. Flatten and mash them together slightly so the pieces will adhere. No two gingerbread men will be alike, and that is part of the fun. Using a large spatula, transfer each cookie to a large cookie sheet that has been lightly greased. Each child's cookie may be marked with a small piece of foil on which his name has been printed with a magic marker.

Bake at 350° for 10 to 15 minutes. Cool and serve with milk during snack time.

Related Activities

Language Arts

Discuss the new words learned, such as knead, dough, ginger, spatula, cinnamon, etc.

Make a bulletin board of the recipe. Read and interpret it to the children. Emphasize the importance of sequential order.

Dramatize the story while cookies are baking to help occupy the waiting time.

Fig. 6.7. "School-made" soup helps to dispel the idea that all soup comes in cans. (Courtesy of South Park Independent School District, Beaumont, Texas.)

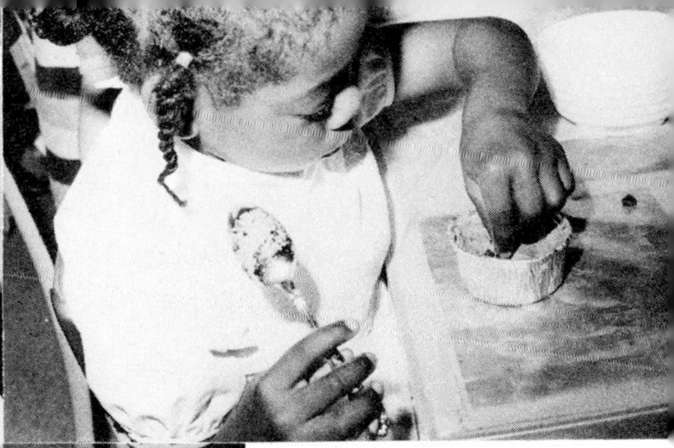

Fig. 6.8. Decorating with chocolate chips is a way of expressing individuality. (Courtesy of Anahuac Independent School District, Anahuac, Texas.)

Fig. 6.9. Making a crumb crust involves all the senses. (Courtesy of Port Arthur, Independent School District, Port Arthur, Texas.)

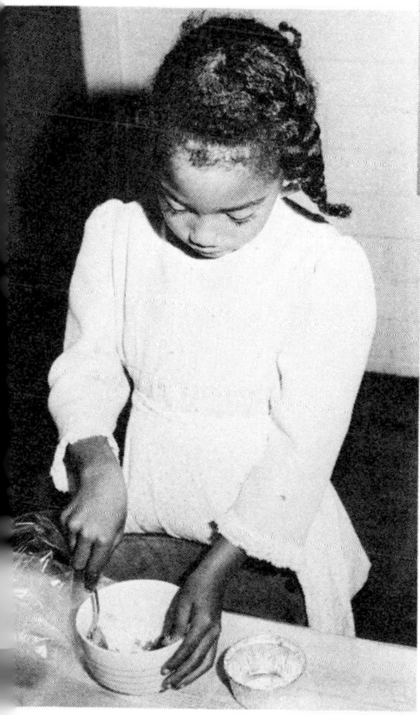

Fig. 6.10. For most children, cooking in the kindergarten will be their first opportunity to become actively involved in the preparation of the food they eat. (Courtesy of Anahuac Independent School District, Anahuac, Texas.)

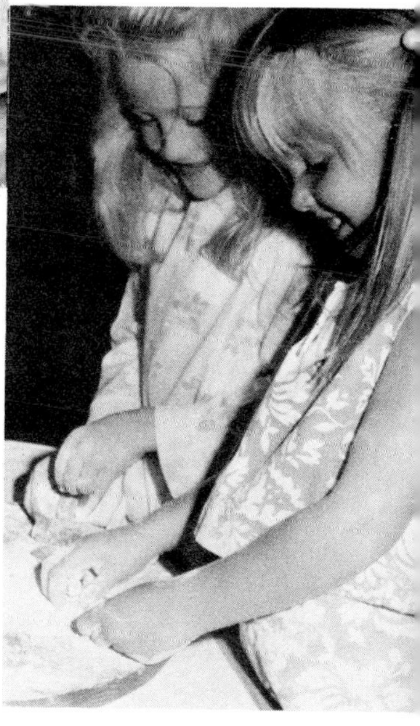

Fig. 6.11. Kindergarten girls make gingerbread men by rolling the dough into small balls. (Courtesy of Don Schwartz and Winette Hogue.)

Social Studies

Work together as a team, share utensils, and take turns. Have students assume responsibility for clean-up. Relate cooperative team efforts to other activities.

Distribute duplicated copies of the recipe.

Science and Mathematics

Help children to measure the ingredients. Study the meaning of "one-half cup."

Set timer for fifteen minutes. Watch clock hands to see if timer and clock coincide.

Show one-to-one correspondence by serving each child his own cookie.

Involve the senses of sight, touch, smell, and taste in preparation and discussion.

Art and Music

Provide clay or play dough for children to re-create the cooking experience.

Cut gingerbread men from brown paper. Mount on colored construction paper. Use as cover for gingerbread recipe to take home.

Play record, *The Gingerbread Man.*

Health and Safety

Stress the importance of cleanliness in cooking and eating.

Emphasize the need for cleaning up spills.

Talk about the new taste of ginger and show children that sampling a new flavor can be an exciting adventure.

Journey Cake, Ho!

Journey Cake, Ho! is an old mountain folk tale about a boy who chases a journey cake that jumped from the oven and ran away. He finally retrieves the cake and also the farm animals that follow the cake. This is a "cumulative" tale based upon repetition and accumulation. Robert McCloskey's humorous illustrations in browns and blues are a perfect backdrop for the lively story.

Since *Journey Cake, Ho!* is a varient of *The Pancake* and *The Gingerbread Man,* the three stories lend themselves to comparison of the content and language.

Journey cake is sometimes known as Johnnycake. Johnnycake was a type of corn bread widely made as this country's frontier was settled. The pioneer food was also sometimes called journey cake, as it could be made with water and taken on long journeys without fear of spoiling. The story is also told that at one time the Indians made such a bread, called Shawnee cake.

Recipe for Journey Cake

1 cup sweet milk
1 cup buttermilk
1 teaspoon salt
1 tablespoon shortening
corn meal
melted butter

Mix first five ingredients together, using enough corn meal to make the batter of a consistency suitable to be rolled into a sheet 1/2 inch thick. Spread the batter on a buttered cookie sheet. Bake in a moderate oven (350°).

As soon as the journey cake begins to brown, baste it with melted butter. Repeat the basting several times until the cake is brown and crispy. Serve while still warm.

Related Activities

Language Arts

Study and compare the three terms Johnnycake, journey cake, and Shawnee cake.

Read *Journey Cake, Ho!* to the children and give them an opportunity to study the illustrations.

Have children discuss the likenesses and differences in the three folk tales, *Journey Cake, Ho!*, *The Pancake*, and *The Gingerbread Man.*

Social Science

Tell the story of Indian corn and how it was ground into meal.

Make a study of different kinds of bread and the people who make them.

Science and Mathematics

Make a chart of the recipe and allow children to use a measuring cup and measuring spoons for the ingredients.

Examine the texture of dry corn meal and compare it with the texture of corn meal after it has been mixed with the liquids.

10. Ruth Sawyer, *Journey Cake, Ho!* (New York: The Viking Press, 1953).

Make journey cake with water instead of milk, store for a few days and then check to see if it is edible. Discuss findings of the experiment.

Bring in some ears of corn for children to examine.

Health and Safety

Discuss the need for refrigeration of many foods. Why would pioneer families need a bread like journey cake?

Locate bread on a chart of the four basic food groups. Discuss the nutritional value of bread.

Have a tasting party and sample many kinds of bread.

Art

Help children make mosaics of dry grains of corn glued on cardboard. These will be more effective if many shapes and colors of grains are used, such as popcorn, yellow corn, Indian corn, etc.

Stone Soup

Stone Soup is an old folk tale in which three hungry French soldiers trick an entire village into providing them with vegetables for their "stone soup."[11]

The gay red and black illustrations are filled with people, animals, and much activity. They serve to give children a glimpse of French village life, and they are organized in such a way that it becomes easy for young children to retell the story.

Recipe for Stone Soup

3 qts. water
1 lb. ground meat
4 carrots, peeled and sliced
4 potatoes, peeled and diced
4 stalks celery, chopped
4 small onions, chopped
1/4 head cabbage
1 can tomatoes, chopped
salt

Simmer ground meat in water 30 minutes (a smooth river-washed agate stone may be added to the water just for fun). Add vegetables and simmer until done. Salt to taste before serving. "Hot" paper cups may be

11. Marcia Brown, *Stone Soup*. (New York: Charles Scribner's Sons, 1947).

used for serving. When salted crackers are served with the soup, it might replace the morning snack.

Related Activities

Language Arts

Read aloud *Stone Soup* and lead a discussion on the meaning of the stone in the soup. Encourage children to explore the battle of wits between the soldiers and the peasants.

Compare the plot, theme, characters, and illustrations in *Stone Soup* with those in *Nail Soup* by Harve Zemach.[12]

Make a vocabulary chart of all the vegetables that children can name. Beside each word, place a rebus drawing to illustrate it.

Arrange pictures of fruits and vegetables into categories on a large chart to give children practice in distinguishing between the two.

Make an arrangement of wax or plastic models of vegetables.

Have children put together jigsaw puzzles of vegetables.

Social Studies

Explain the meaning of the term "folk tale."

Discuss the houses, clothing, and cobblestone streets pictured in the illustrations.

Allow children to express their opinions about what magic the stone brought to the soup.

Make a study of vegetables from the garden to the dining table. Consider all the people who work to make vegetables available to the consumer.

Provide an opportunity in the playhouse center for boys and girls to re-create the story of Stone Soup.

Science and Mathematics

Help children to discover that vegetables have different sizes, colors, shapes, textures, smells, and flavors.

Have children count out salted crackers to go with the soup.

Health and Safety

Categorize foods into the four basic food groups needed for good nutrition. Show that vegetables, in some form, should be eaten everyday.

Art

Use air-hardening clay to model different vegetables. When dry, paint each the appropriate color with tempera paint.

12. Harve Zemach, *Nail Soup* (Chicago: Follett Publishing Co., 1964).

Nail Soup

Nail Soup is a Swedish folk tale about a tramp who asks a rather selfish old woman for food. He is told that there is not a bite in the house. The tramp declares he will make soup for both of them. He puts water in a pot and drops in a nail. When he needs meat, potatoes, and other vegetables to make it a "feast fit for the king and queen," the old woman happens to "remember" where she has hidden these ingredients.

When the delicious soup is eaten and the tramp starts to leave, the woman tells him, "And thank you for teaching me how to make soup with a nail, because now that I know how, I shall always live in comfort."

"That's all right," said the tramp. "It's easy if you remember to add something good to it."[13]

Recipe for Nail Soup

3 qts. water
1 lb. ground meat
4 carrots, peeled and sliced
4 potatoes, peeled and diced
4 stalks celery, chopped
4 small onions, chopped
1/4 head cabbage
1 can tomatoes, chopped

Simmer ground meat in water 30 minutes (a large aluminum nail may be added to the water just for fun). Add vegetables and simmer until done. Salt to taste. "Hot" paper cups may be used for serving. The soup, accompanied by crackers, might replace the morning snack.

Related Activities

Language Arts

Read *Nail Soup* to the children at storytime. Lead a discussion of the trickery involved. Help children to see that the tramp was able to make the old woman a little less selfish.

Allow children to express their ideas about the value of the nail in the soup.

Discuss the humor in the title *Nail Soup.*

Social Science

Study the illustrations and discuss the clothing worn by the characters.

13. Ibid.

Talk about what the old woman meant when she said, "Such people don't grow on trees."

Science and Mathematics

Estimate the time it will take to bring the water to a boil. Time the water by a clock in the classroom.

Test the water with a food thermometer while the water is cold and then after it begins to boil. Show children the difference in the two readings.

Play a tasting game with raw vegetables. Wrap small pieces of carrot, potato, celery, onion, green pepper, and cabbage individually in plastic wrap and place together in a mixing bowl. Each child, with eyes closed, reaches in and chooses a piece. Without looking, he unwraps and tastes it (eats it, if he wishes) and then guesses what it is. Let three groups of children play this game at once to shorten the time each child must wait for a turn. Evaluate the game by showing that tasting new foods can be an exciting adventure.

Health and Safety

Teach safety precautions to be observed in using a knife and vegetable parer. A plastic knife with serrated edge is a safe tool for children to use.

Emphasize the necessity of washing raw vegetables before eating them.

Art

Make a large collage of vegetable pictures cut from magazines and seed catalogues.

The Carrot Seed

In the face of discouragement from his parents and from his big brother, a small boy plants a carrot seed. "It won't come up. It won't come up," they tell him; but every day he sprinkles the ground with water and, sure enough, it *does* come up.[14]

This is an excellent book to use with young children because it shows them as they are—incurable optimists.

Recipe for Buttered Carrots

Wash eight to ten carrots and remove outer surface with vegetable parer. Place carrots on chopping board and slice (teacher activity). Run

14. Ruth Krauss, *The Carrot Seed* (New York: Harper & Row, Publishers, 1966). Available in paperback from Scholastic Book Services, New York.

two inches of water into sauce pan. Add one teaspoon salt. Place pan over high heat and bring to boil. Add carrot slices. Cover with lid and lower heat. Cook fifteen minutes or until tender. Pierce with fork to test tenderness. Drain. Empty carrots into bowl. Dot with plenty of butter and salt to taste. Serve while still warm.

Related Activities

Language Arts

Read *The Carrot Seed* to the children. Give them a chance to express their ideas about the story.

Take apart a paperback edition of the book. Let children put the pages in sequential order on the chalk ledge. Help them retell the story.

Move from concrete to abstract by showing a real carrot, a model of a carrot, a picture of a carrot, and finally the word "carrot."

Social Science

If possible, make a field trip to the grocery store to buy the carrots. Talk to the grocer and ask him to leave on the tops. Look at the other vegetables in the store. Find out how many of them the children recognize by name.

Encourage children to express their feelings about the little boy as he waits and waits for the seed to come up. Also let them describe their feelings about the ending of the story when he hauls his carrot home in a wheelbarrow!

Listen to the record of *The Carrot Seed.*

Science and Mathematics

Make a collection of seeds, from the smallest, such as carrot seeds, to the largest, such as coconuts. Display them in graduated order from smallest to largest.

Make a collection of seed catalogues.

Plant the tops of the carrots, cut side down, in a dish of water.

Study the vegetable page in picture dictionaries.

Classify pictures of vegetables that grow below the ground, and vegetables that grow above ground.

Health and Safety

Review safety precautions to observe when cooking is in progress.

Locate carrots on a chart of the four basic food groups.

Make an effort to improve children's attitudes about eating vegetables.

Art

Make pictures of carrots.

Dip twelve-inch pieces of yarn in liquid starch and help each child to arrange a piece into the shape of a carrot on a piece of cardboard. When thoroughly dry, let them paint the carrot bright orange with a green top. These can be mounted on a bulletin board labeled, "We Like Carrots."

The Egg Tree

Easter traditions in a Pennsylvania Dutch family are the theme of this book. It is an entertaining story of cooking, decorating, hiding, hunting, and eating Easter eggs. Directions are given for making the lovely Easter egg tree.

The Egg Tree is a story of adventure, fun, and excitement, but it is also a book of art. The pages are decorated with authentic Pennsylvania Dutch designs created by the author. Even the pre-reading child can enjoy an aesthetic experience just by turning through the pages. Katherine Milhous won the Caldecott Award for *The Egg Tree* in 1951.[15]

Recipe for Easter Eggs

Place one dozen clean white eggs gently into a large saucepan. Add cold water until it is one-half inch above top of eggs. Cover with lid. Heat slowly to boiling. Turn heat very low. Cook twenty minutes. Place pan in sink. Run cool water over eggs until they are cool enough to handle. Eggs are now ready for dyeing or painting.

Related Activities

Language Arts

Study the book *The Egg Tree* and prepare the story for telling. It may be necessary to abbreviate it somewhat for young children.

Provide children time and opportunity to study the illustrations.

Make plans to create an egg tree for the classroom. Prepare invitations to be sent to parents and friends. The teacher might duplicate the notes and then let children decorate them with Easter designs.

Social Science

Discuss the Pennsylvania Dutch folk art as it appears on the borders of the pages in *The Egg Tree.*

Invite friends in to see the egg tree as did the Pennsylvania Dutch.

15. Katherine Milhous, *The Egg Tree* (New York: Charles Scribner's Sons, 1950).

Science and Mathematics

Break a raw egg into a dish and encourage children to examine it. Break one of the cooked eggs and examine it. Discuss what happened in the cooking process.

Count the eggs and study the concept of "a dozen." Count the spaces in an empty egg carton.

Count out six eggs and study the concept of "one-half dozen." Cover one-half the spaces in an egg carton and count the remaining spaces.

Health and Safety

Discuss the need for refrigerating eggs.

Review safety precautions to be observed while eggs are cooking on the hot plate in the classroom.

Illustrate the fact that eggs are included in the four basic food groups.

Art

Practice making Pennsylvania Dutch designs by using those in *The Egg Tree* as a guide. Mount on the bulletin board.

Use wax crayons to make designs on the cooked eggs before dipping them in vegetable dye or before painting them with water colors. The wax will resist the dye, and the designs will show through. The children can make polka dots, stripes, and zigzag designs.

Make an egg tree by letting children cut and color paper eggs to hang on a branch that has been wedged into a flower pot. Have children bring Easter toys from home to place under the tree, just as the children did in *The Egg Tree.*

Rain Makes Applesauce

This picture book was named a runner-up for the coveted Caldecott Award in 1965. The lovely, ethereal illustrations are a perfect complement to a book of nonsense with its silly talk for young listeners. The language patterns are delightful and children love to repeat the refrain, "O, you're just talking silly talk." They recognize the nonsense as very similar to the silly talk they like to make up and say to each other.

The nonsense in *Rain Makes Applesauce* is balanced with the necessary realism to make it palatable to children. Hidden in the lower right-hand corner of each nonsense drawing is a small segment of the true story of applesauce. The sequence begins with the planting of an apple tree and ends with the making and eating of applesauce. An excellent book for reading aloud and for rereading many times.[16]

Recipe for Applesauce

6 sour apples
2/3 cup white granulated sugar
1 cup water

Wash apples and cut them into quarters. Use a cutting board and show children how to cut away from themselves. Since cutting must be closely supervised, allow only a few children to work at one time. Carefully remove cores. Put apples and sugar in saucepan. Add 1 cup water. Cover with lid. Cook slowly 30 minutes or until tender. Stir occasionally. Cool. Press through a colander. A few drops of red coloring may be added to make a rosy red applesauce. Serve on graham crackers at snack time. Note: It is not necessary to peel the apples.

Related Activities

Language Arts

For comparison purposes, have on hand pictures of apples, wax and plastic models, and real apples (include some yellow ones). Make a list of all the adjectives children use in describing the pictures, the models, and the real apples. Read all the words on the list back to the children.

Write the word "apple" on chart paper and have children cut apples from seed catalogues to paste on the chart.

Social Science

Take a field trip to a grocery store to survey the various apple products available. Buy a few to bring back to the room for sampling.

Science and Mathematics

Discuss and illustrate the meaning of "quarter."

Measure 2/3 cup of sugar in measuring cup.

Measure one cup water in measuring cup.

Have children count the apples.

Using apples of different sizes, show "greater than," "smaller than," etc.

Sample apple juice and apple butter. Discuss difference in consistency.

16. Julian Scheer, *Rain Makes Applesauce* (New York: Holiday House, 1964).

Art

Make a large tree for the bulletin board and allow children to cut paper apples to hang on it.

White Snow Bright Snow

This is a beautifully illustrated and poetic story of a big snow, written by Alvin Tresselt. From the falling of the first lacy flakes to the point where everything is buried under the white drifts, people go about their appointed tasks. Adults are busy making preparations for being shut in, but the children build a snowman.

Spring finally arrives and brings an end to the big snow: fence posts lose their dunce caps, the snowman's arms drop off, and running water gurgles in gutters and rain pipes.

The brilliant colors of the houses against the white snow and blue sky helped to win the Caldecott Award for Roger Duvoisin, the illustrator.[17]

Recipe for a Snowman Cake

1 box white cake mix
Seven-minute frosting mix
1 can shredded coconut
assorted gumdrops
candy cane

Mix white cake according to directions on the box and bake in two 8-inch round pans. Cool. Arrange the cakes together on a tray. One cake forms the head of the snowman and the other the body.

Frost the cakes with frosting mix (or seven-minute frosting) and sprinkle generously with coconut. Make buttons, eyes, nose, and mouth from gumdrops. Cut the snowman a top hat from black paper and fasten on with toothpicks. Add a big candy cane for trim.

Related Activities

Language Arts

Read *White Snow Bright Snow* to the children. Lead a discussion centered around the building of a snowman.

17. Alvin Tresselt, *White Snow Bright Snow* (New York: Lothrop, Lee & Shephard Co., Inc., 1947).

Read *The Snowy Day* by Ezra Keats[18] and *Frosty the Snowman,* retold by Annie North Bedford.[19] Compare the snowmen in these two books with the one in *White Snow Bright Snow.*

Play the record of *Frosty the Snowman,* and help the children to learn the words of the song.

Social Science

Show pictures of the postman, the policeman, the farmer, and the housewife. Talk about their work. What kinds of jobs would they do to prepare for a storm?

On a large wall map of the United States, point out the areas where snowfall is the heaviest. Locate the warmer zones where snow is seldom seen. Help children to find their own state on the map and talk about the average amount of snowfall in that particular part of the country.

Compile a scrapbook of snow scenes from newspapers, magazines, travel folders, and post cards.

Make booklets about the snowman cake (including the recipe) for children to take home. Let each child draw and color a picture of the snowman cake as a cover for his booklet.

Invite another kindergarten or first grade class in to share the snowman cake. If cut in small squares, it will serve thirty-five to forty children.

If the school cafeteria oven is used for baking the cake, write a thank-you note to the manager. The teacher can serve as recorder for the children's sentences.

18. Ezra Jack Keats, *The Snowy Day* (New York: Viking, 1962).
19. Annie North Bedford, *Frosty the Snowman* (New York: Golden Press, 1950).

Fig. 6.12 and 6.13. After reading several books about snow, these children created their own version of a snowman. (Courtesy of Winette Hogue and Donald Schwartz.)

Science and Mathematics

Count the strokes used in mixing the cake batter.

Show children the baking temperature printed on the cake mix box. Write the numeral on the chalkboard. Show them how an adult would set the oven thermostat accordingly.

Point out the baking time printed on the cake mix box. Write the numeral on the chalkboard. Set the alarm clock to go off at the end of the baking period. Illustrate how an adult would set the oven timer.

The teacher or a lunchroom cook can show the children how to test for doneness.

Health and Safety

Emphasize the danger of working near a hot oven. Let children examine the asbestos-lined mittens used for removing hot pans from the ovens. Allow children to watch removal of hot cakes from the oven.

Art

Paint a mural of *White Snow Bright Snow.* Use a strip of black tar paper from the lumber yard. Spread it on the floor. With white chalk, draw a base line the full length of the tar paper about six inches from the bottom. Mix tempera paint in one-pound coffee cans to the consistency of thick cream.

Using large soft brushes, let each child paint a house on the base line. Emphasize the fact that everything on a mural should be *large.*

When the houses are completely dry, the children can pile "snow" on the roofs by using thick white tempera paint. White dots of paint may be sprinkled over the entire mural to simulate snowflakes.

The brilliantly colored houses and white snow will stand out against the black background and children can experience the satisfaction of working together to create a beautiful snow scene.

7

"Know Thyself": Books for Bibliotherapy

Printed in a child's writing on the title page of a copy of *Charlotte's Web* were found the words, "So dear to my heart." The words were left there as the young reader's tribute to Wilbur and Charlotte, and as a kind of quiet response to the story's impact. A book that has the ability to evoke such sincere expression of emotion has undoubtedly given the child new insight into himself. Such highly personal interaction between a reader and literature is what is meant by the term "bibliotherapy." This practice of using literature to help students solve their personal problems and to assist them in meeting the basic needs of growth and development is not a new one. To some extent, teachers have always used it.

Even though the implications of bibliotherapy are psychological, it is not suggested that the classroom teacher become a psychoanalyst. "On the other hand, every teacher and librarian can and should make a concerted effort to know the needs of their students; to know the kind of humanistic literature that can enrich the lives of young people and give them insight into their problems."[1]

1. Betty Coody, "Bibliotherapy: Using Books to Meet Needs," *Teaching in the 70's*, by Kenneth Briggs (Dubuque, Iowa: Kendall/Hunt Publishing Co., 1971), p. 60.

An imminent psychologist has recommended that there should exist bookstores dedicated to handling and promoting bibliotherapeutic materials—shelves stocked with humanistic books, journals, and pamphlets.[2] Even though such bookstores may not yet exist, there are many excellent books available that portray real people solving and adjusting to problems of personal appearance, physical handicaps, social acceptance, neglect and deprivation, poverty, war, prejudice, and other problems that are so crucial in the lives of today's children. Such books exist because the author had a story to tell, not a sermon to preach:

> Bibliotherapy does not refer to the use of didactic literature that hammers home a moral lesson, but, rather, it takes advantage of books in which true-to-life people (or animals as people substitutes) resolve conflicts, overcome handicaps, and make satisfactory adjustments to life. If the reader is able to learn something from their experiences, well and good.[3]

Huck and Kuhn set forth standards by which a book might be considered "humanistic." They tell us that literature is suitable for bibliotherapy if it tells an interesting story and yet has the power to help a reader (1) acquire information and knowledge about the psychology and physiology of human behavior, (2) learn what it means to "know thyself," (3) find an interest outside himself, (4) relieve conscious problems in a controlled manner, (5) utilize an opportunity for identification and compensation, and (6) illuminate difficulties and acquire insight into his own behavior.[4]

Bibliotherapy is based on the principle that through empathy with characters he meets in books, a reader is able to know and understand more about himself. In a character's strengths and weaknesses, the reader recognizes his own. When a book character's behavior causes him to fail or to succeed, the reader recognizes his own personality characteristics and is in a position to make necessary adjustments. It is possible for him to be much more objective and analytical about the book character's problems than about his own. Ego damage is not so threatening in the vicarious experience as in the real one. Smith and Dechant write:

> An identification with the characters of literature allows the individual to relive elements of his own past experience and attain new understandings of them. For example, it may allow him to look at fic-

2. Abraham H. Maslow, *Toward a Psychology of Being* (Princeton, N. J.: D. Van Nostrand Co., Inc., 1968), p. 240.
3. Coody, op. cit., p. 61.
4. Charlotte S. Huck and Doris Young Kuhn, *Children's Literature in the Elementary School,* 2nd ed. (New York: Holt, Rinehart & Winston, Inc., 1968), p. 264.

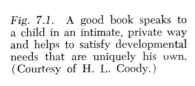

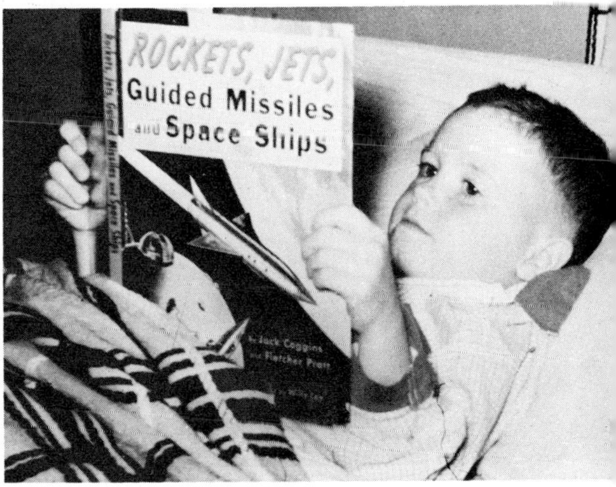

Fig. 7.1. A good book speaks to a child in an intimate, private way and helps to satisfy developmental needs that are uniquely his own. (Courtesy of H. L. Coody.)

tional mothers and fathers and thus gain a better understanding of his own parents. Or he sees, through a character portrayal, the reactions (and the reasons for those reactions) of other persons to his own personality traits.[5]

A teacher should know hundreds of such books to be made available to young children—old books and new that express man's highest thoughts stated in the best possible manner and illustrated with the finest art. In this country, there is no shortage of quality literature for children. There is, however, evidence that many teachers are oblivious to its potential for enriching the lives of children and for giving them a more positive self-image.

Ozman conducted a research study concerned with the values reflected in children's readers (textbooks) at the primary level and the relationship of these to educational philosophy. He concluded: "The results of this study seem to indicate that a value analysis of children's reading material should not be limited to basal readers, but should include all of the kinds of reading material utilized in the classroom at all levels."[6] It was his opinion that books used by children cause them to adopt certain value attitudes. If his is a valid judgement, and textbooks do exert enough impact on primary children to influence the formulation of values, it is easy to imagine the capability of books that have greater literary merit. It is

5. Henry P. Smith and Emerald V. Dechant, *Psychology in Teaching Reading* (Englewood Cliffs, N. J.: Prentice-Hall, Inc., 1961), p. 314.

6. Howard A. Ozman, Jr., "Value Implications in Children's Reading Material," *The Reading Teacher* 22 (1968):243-250.

most unfortunate when the only book a teacher knows well is a textbook. According to Meeker:

> No teacher can get along without books, for books and children belong together. The books should present few words, but large colorful pictures, or pictures which so well illustrate the stories and rhymes that a child can follow with his eyes what he has heard with his ears. Books build new understandings, they unlock the imagination, they are indispensible for reading readiness. They should include country and city life, animal life, history, fantasy, and the brotherhood of man, regardless of race, creed or color.[7]

Without doubt, a new emphasis is needed in many programs of reading readiness and beginning reading, with literature taking its rightful place in the young child's curriculum. If some of the time used for textbook and workbook exercises has to be sacrificed in the process, then so be it. "Children must value the reading process not as a mere ability to translate symbols on a page, but as a tool for intelligent living."[8]

For reading to bring a lifetime of pleasure, stimulation, and comfort to a person, the foundation must be established during the years of early childhood. In addition to teaching the skills of reading, a teacher of young children must find time for telling stories, reading aloud, presenting picture books, dramatizing characters, and for countless other procedures that afford children happy encounters with books. According to Cianciolo:

> A teacher of literature or reading must teach the students to make judgments about the literature. The judgments at the beginning will refer to the content of the book; they will refer to the experiences and values that the book offers them. Literature should present designs for development of personal and interpersonal values that are commonly accepted by the general society as ideal and satisfying.[9]

Because the motivation of children is a result of their efforts to meet needs, it is imperative that the teacher of early childhood understand the characteristics of those basic needs. Effective use of bibliotherapy depends on the teacher's knowledge of children's literature and an awareness of the way in which children grow and develop. It also demands that a teacher care enough to seek out the right book at the right time.

7. Alice M. Meeker, *Enjoying Literature with Children* (New York: The Odyssey Press, 1969), p. 20.
8. Donald W. Pfau, "Effects of Planned Recreational Reading Programs," *The Reading Teacher* 21 (1967):35.
9. Patricia Jean Cianciolo, "A Recommended Reading Diet for Children," *Elementary English* 48 (1971):787.

The Basic Needs

Every normal child has certain basic needs in life—needs which indicate that something vital must be supplied if he is to be a functional, well-adjusted, and happy individual. Each person spends a lifetime striving to satisfy needs, and the state of his mental health depends on how successfully the task is accomplished.

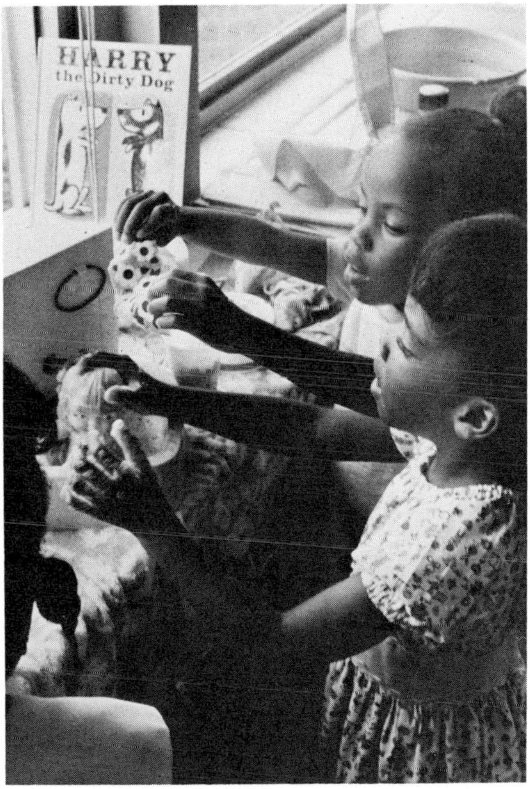

Fig. 7.2. Harry the Dirty Dog inspires these two kindergarten girls to wash their dolls with soap and water. (Courtesy of South Park Independent School District, Beaumont, Texas.)

The classroom teacher sensitive to "need theory" is one who recognizes that the behavior of children does not just happen. It is caused. Maslow's theory of motivation holds that all human behavior can be explained in terms of the activity generated in satisfying the basic needs. He organizes these needs into five fundamental groups: (1) physiological needs, (2) safety needs, (3) love and belonging needs, (4) esteem needs, and (5) self-actualization needs.[10]

Physiological Needs

Most of man's waking moments are spent in the struggle to meet the overwhelming desire for food, drink, and shelter, the creature comforts of life. To the teacher of young children, this means that "the basic needs of food, clothing, rest and affection must be met before efficient school learning can take place. The effective school curriculum will contain provisions for these necessary ingredients."[11]

Some children are forced to spend their entire childhood outside the warm world of security. "These are the children who cannot be sure of the basic necessities. Will there be enough food? Is there someone to take care of you? There is uncertainty in their lives about whom they really belong to. Who is the father? And is the mother available to the child in important mothering ways? In fact, is there anybody who really cares about this child in a deep and important way?"[12] After painting a large bowl of fruit on her art paper, a second-grade girl wrote at the bottom: "Happiness is when my daddy has a job."

It would be ludicrous, of course, to imply that books can relieve the suffering of a child who is hungry and fraught with anxiety. Obviously, other measures are needed in such cases. Books can, however, help a child to understand that the struggle for security is universal and timeless. And book characters can provide examples of what people have been able to accomplish in the mundane and often weary process of earning a living. In Ellis Credle's book, *Down, Down the Mountain,* two children of the Blue Ridge Mountains raise and sell turnips to buy new shoes for themselves, and in the process find adventure and self-reliance. From ancient folk tales to modern stories, this struggle for material security is a popular theme. It is a theme that is particularly appealing to children because of its infinite reality in their lives.

Safety Needs

A child's feeling of safety may be threatened by any situation that jeopardizes his well-being. He is easily frightened by strange people, sur-

10. Abraham H. Maslow, "A Theory of Human Motivation," *Psychological Review* 50 (1943):370-396.

11. Joe L. Frost and Glenn R. Hawkes, eds., *The Disadvantaged Child, Issues and Innovations* (Boston: Houghton Mifflin Co., 1966), p. 248.

12. Barbara Biber, *Young Deprived Children and Their Educational Needs* (Washington, D. C.: Association for Childhood Education International, 1967), p. 11.

roundings, and activities. Such dangers to his safety may be real or imagined; it makes little difference to the child. He instinctively tries to protect himself from the hazards as best he can.

Maintaining an environment where the safety needs of young children can be gratified is an ethical responsibility of the classroom teacher. By adhering to a certain amount of routine in the daily program and by being a predictable person on whom the child can depend, it is quite possible for the teacher to shield a child from many of the threats to his safety. Keeping a delicate balance between the variety needed to create interest, and the routine needed to provide security, is one of the most important skills a teacher of early childhood can acquire.

Children, as well as adults, fear crime, pollution, disease, poverty, and war as ominous threats to their well-being. Unfortunately, no teacher has the power to protect children from these harbingers of pain, but any teacher who cares can help a child to develop the inner strength to live courageously with elements of danger and not be devastated by them. Taro Yashima, author-illustrator of some of the finest books we have for helping children cope with their problems, said of his work:

> I would like to continue publishing picture books for children until my life ends. The theme for all those should be, needless to say, "Let children enjoy living on this earth, let children be strong enough not to be beaten or twisted by evil on this earth."[13]

Yashima's philosophy shines forth in all his writing and painting, and even the youngest children are able to sense the beauty and meaning in them. By endowing Crow Boy with the strength to rise above ridicule and prejudice, to find an honorable place for himself in the world, Yashima deliberately and consciously tries to give his readers the same inner strength to sustain them in times of crisis.

Love and Belonging Needs

Every child needs desperately to love someone and to have someone love him in return. The family unit is the first source of love and affection for most children, but unfortunately many children exist in a world where love is totally lacking. For such children the school of early childhood should become a refuge where affectionate relationships with adults and peers may compensate, to some extent, for the love that is denied at home.

Adults who work with children must always be ready to give an extra measure of love and understanding to a child who needs it, and should

13. Muriel Fuller, ed., *More Junior Authors* (New York: The H. W. Wilson Co., 1963), p. 231.

find ways to help him gain acceptance by groups of children his own age. To leave such matters to chance is to foreordain that some children will remain outsiders, perhaps for the rest of their lives. "In our society the thwarting of these love needs is the most commonly found core in cases of maladjustment and more severe psychopathology."[14]

Certainly a child's literature should reflect warm, affectionate, loving relationships between people. Such books can help the more fortunate

Fig. 7.3. A child's literature should reflect warm, affectionate, loving relationships between people. (Courtesy of South Park Independent School District, Beaumont, Texas.)

child to appreciate his circumstances and to be more sensitive to the love and belonging needs of others. The same books can help the deprived child to learn about giving and receiving love in generous and accepting ways, just as Wanda Petronski in *The Hundred Dresses* was able to bring a new awareness and compassion to the girls who taunted her about the faded cotton dress she wore to school every day. *Where the Wild Things Are, Apt. 3, Little Chief,* and *Ask Mr. Bear* are other examples of books that portray the struggle for love, and the ultimate achievement of acceptance.

Esteem Needs

Within every child is a strong desire to feel worthy, to know that he has value, importance and status, first in the immediate family, next in the

14. Raymond F. Gale, *Developmental Behavior, A Humanistic Approach* (New York: The Macmillan Co., 1969), p. 105.

extended family, and finally in groups outside the family. He longs to have his feelings, ideas, and opinions respected by others. He often goes to great lengths to prove to himself that it is so.

A child's sense of esteem is closely linked to his achievement and competency. To gain a sense of self-respect, he needs to be successful in many of the ventures he undertakes, at least during the first few years of life. He also requires a reputation among others regarding his unique ability to perform certain skills and tasks in an adequate, perhaps even superior manner. Crow Boy gained recognition and respect with his unusual ability to imitate the voices of crows. Helping a rejected child to acquire competency in some area is frequently all that is needed to gain him an entrée into peer groups.

As a child matures, he learns from life how to control his behavior and by doing so, to influence his environment. He also strengthens this understanding by associating with characters in literature who work to accomplish something worthy of respect, often in the face of many failures and setbacks. Such books as *The Little Engine that Could, Pelle's New Suit, Whistle for Willie, Yonie Wondernose,* and *Benjie On His Own* clearly depict heroes who achieve in spite of the odds against them. Children who come to know such characters in an intimate way are able to draw sustenance and inspiration from them over and over again. Many college students admit that they still say to themselves on occasion, "I think I can, I think I can." Georgiou describes the kind of books that have the power to move children in such deep and lasting ways:

> Books that reveal the skill and affection that have gone into their writing are books that speak to each individual in the personal, private voice of a friend. And it is with this friendship that a book, whether fact or fiction, establishes a world the child can join, learn from, and grow in; a world where he too can laugh, weep, rebel, and cherish.[15]

The Need for Self-Actualization

Closely akin to the need for esteem is the need to become a self-actualizing person. "Even when all other needs are reasonably well fulfilled, a person is discontented and restless unless he is doing that for which he is best fitted. This desire for self-fulfillment, in essence, is the need to become what one is capable of becoming."[16]

A child moves in the direction of self-actualization as he sets goals for himself and then works toward those goals. Some goals he accomplishes;

15. Constantine Georgiou, *Children and Their Literature* (Englewood Cliffs, N. J.: Prentice-Hall, Inc., 1969), p. 6.

16. Kenneth H. Hoover and Paul M. Hollingsworth, *Learning and Teaching in the Elementary School* (Boston: Allyn & Bacon, Inc., 1970), p. 9.

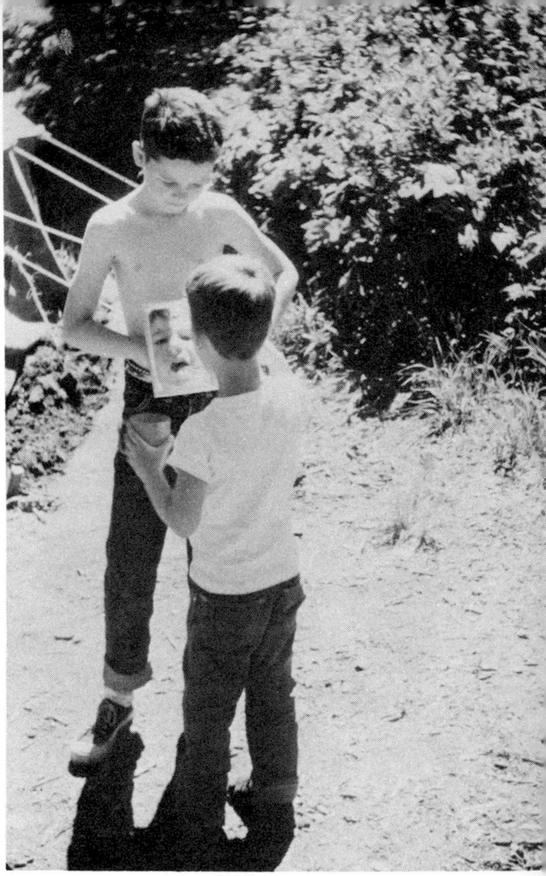

Fig. 7.4. By a firsthand involvement with nature, a child begins to understand the individual's role in environmental problems. Related experiences with literature serve to reinforce and synthesize the learning. (Courtesy of Winette Hogue.)

Fig. 7.5. Children gain a sensitivity to their natural environment by living in it and by exploring it, but books that state ecological problems factually and clearly help them see the need for preserving it for others. (Courtesy of H. L. Coody.)

others he fails to reach. Some of his goals are altered or abandoned along the way. But the aims are the child's own, no matter what objectives others have in mind for him. "Each person illuminates and refines his goals as he works conscientiously and intelligently at a task, and one person's goals cannot be transferred to another."[17]

One significant way in which a child seeks to actualize himself is by setting goals that align him with causes and issues that he considers important. "We have a deep capacity of caring for others, for protecting, encouraging, and for helping *them* grow and to find meaning and satisfaction in their lives. If we do not use this capacity we feel incomplete and unsatisfied."[18]

It is a mistake to assume that young children are not capable of thinking seriously about life or that they are unaware of the problems that exist in our society. Even young children are not exempt from personal conflicts. Neither are they oblivious to problems arising out of group relation-

17. Clyde Inez Martin, *An Elementary School Social Studies Program* (Austin: The University of Texas Press, 1963), p. 26.
18. Gale, op. cit., pp. 115-116.

ships. They are more concerned about environmental problems than are most adults. Books have the power to direct their boundless creative energy into causes that lead to self-realization while helping other people. Mildred A. Dawson says of literature teachers:

> We can build lifetime interests, provide future adults with a soul-satisfying means of recreation in the leisuretime hours ahead, build an inclination to find answers to personal problems by turning to the philosophers and perceptive expressers of wise action.[19]

A. A. Milne captured the essence of bibliotherapy long before the term was coined. Once Pooh Bear visited Rabbit and ate so much honey that he became wedged in the hole on his way out:

> Bear began to sigh, and then found he couldn't because he was so tightly stuck; and a tear rolled down his eye, as he said: "Then would you read a Sustaining Book, such as would help and comfort a Wedged Bear in Great Tightness?" So for a week Christopher Robin read that sort of book at the North end of Pooh. . . .[20]

All too often during a child's lifetime he finds himself in a great tightness. It is a good friend who will hand him a sustaining book, or better yet, read one to him. Any teacher who recognizes a child's problem, pinpoints a book that might be helpful and brings the two together in an unobtrusive manner is not only a good friend to the child, but is, at the same time, operating at a high level of professionalism.

CHILDREN'S BOOKS FOR BIBLIOTHERAPY

Personal Problems

Ask Mr. Bear, by Marjorie Flack. New York: The Macmillan Co., 1932. Danny wonders what to give his mother for her birthday. The hen, the goose, the goat, the sheep, and the cow take him to ask Mr. Bear. Mr. Bear has a wonderful solution.

Benjie On His Own, written by Joan Lexau and illustrated by Don Bolognese. New York: The Dial Press, 1970. Old enough to be in school for the first time, Benjie is faced with the problem of finding his way home in the large crowded city. He finds that independence can be both painful and pleasant.

Felice, written and illustrated by Marcia Brown. New York: Charles Scribner's Sons, 1958. The heartwarming story of a young Italian boy named Gino, and his cat, Felice. The author-illustrator paints a watercolor portrait of the city of Venice with its gondolas and barcas loaded with fruits, vegetables, flowers, and coal for the market.

19. Mildred A. Dawson, "Oral Interpretation," *Elementary English* 45 (1968):287.
20. A. A. Milne, *The World of Pooh* (New York: E. P. Dutton & Co., Inc., 1957), pp. 32-33.

Gilberto and the Wind, written and illustrated by Marie Hall Ets. New York: The Viking Press, 1963. A small Mexican-American boy has many experiences with both harsh and kindly winds. A good story for preschool and kindergarten children.

In My Mother's House, written by Ann Nolan Clark and illustrated by Velino Herrera. New York: The Viking Press, 1941. A poetic book written from an Indian child's point of view. Tewa Indian children of Sante Fe, New Mexico assisted the author in writing about the everyday things that are so important in their lives. Illustrated with authentic Indian designs.

Jonathan, written by Eleanor Graham Vance and illustrated by Albert John Pucci. Chicago: Follett Publishing Co., 1966. Four-year-old Jonathan has many questions about nature and about himself. Finally, he finds a wise Answer Man who not only gives him accurate information, but does it in lilting verse. Excellent for reading aloud to preschoolers.

Juanita, written and illustrated by Leo Politi. New York: Charles Scribner's Sons, 1948. Juanita celebrates her fourth birthday in the Mexican custom with cake, candles, and cascarones. Her gift is a live dove. On the day before Easter Sunday, "The Blessing of the Animals" takes place, and Juanita's dove receives a blessing. The Politi style of illustration is reminiscent of the great mural painters of Mexico.

Whistle for Willie, written and illustrated by Ezra Jack Keats. New York: The Viking Press, 1964. Peter, a small black boy, accomplishes the important task of learning to whistle. Now he will be able to call his dog, Willie. A realistic story of patient effort and achievement.

Yonie Wondernose, written and illustrated by Marguerite de Angeli. Garden City, N. Y.: Doubleday & Co., Inc., 1944. Circumstances cause Yonie, a seven-year-old Pennsylvania Dutch boy, to assume responsibility for taking care of his grandmother, his mother and sisters. His problems are compounded when lightning strikes the barn and the animals have to be evacuated. An exciting story of an Amish boy's growing maturity.

Interpersonal Problems

Apt. 3, written and illustrated by Ezra Jack Keats. New York: The Macmillan Co., 1971. On a rainy afternoon, Sam and his little brother walk down the halls of the apartment building where they live, listening to the many sounds of life behind closed doors. Beautiful harmonica music comes from Apt. 3. The musician is a blind man who becomes their new friend. Each page is a beautiful painting.

Little Chief, written and illustrated by Syd Hoff. New York: Harper & Row, Publishers, 1961. Little Chief has only animals for friends until the wagon train brings other children to the green valley. The children share games and teach the adults how to live together in harmony. An easy-to-read book.

Nannabah's Friend, written by Mary Perrine and illustrated by Leonard Weisgard. Boston: Houghton Mifflin Co., 1970. Nannabah dreads the day when she will be old enough to take the sheep into the canyon alone. Herding sheep is a lonely, frightening job for a small girl. Her grandfather says a Navajo prayer "to help you when you walk alone." Nannabah proves her courage and eventually makes friends with another young shepherdess in the canyon.

The New Pet, written and illustrated by Marjorie Flack. Garden City, N. Y.: Doubleday & Co., Inc., 1943. Dick and Judy beg for a pet—a dog, a cat, a rabbit, fish or parakeet. But the pet turns out to be a baby brother. Judy says: "Timmy isn't like a dog or a bird or a rabbit or a fish. Timmy is just like me!" A story suitable for three- and four-year-olds.

Paz, written by Cheli Duran Ryan and illustrated by Nonny Hogrogian. New York: The Macmillan Co., 1971. Because Balthazar and Therese Paz wish to live in peace and neutrality between two countries at war with each other, they build a high rock wall around their home and declare it an independent country. Soon men, women and children are climbing over the wall into Paz. Eventually the peaceful influence of Paz brings a settlement between the two fighting countries, and the wall is torn down.

Too Many Sisters, written by Jerrold Beim and illustrated by Dick Dodge. New York: William Morrow and Co., 1956. The story of boys rejecting girls from their clubhouse and finally accepting them because of the contributions they make in a crisis. The boys resolve that even the pioneers had allowed ladies to come into their forts.

Two Is a Team, written by Lorraine and Jerrold Beim and illustrated by Ernest Crichlow. New York: Harcourt Brace Jovanovich, Inc., 1945. As the title implies, two boys settle their differences and pool resources to build a wagon they need in their job as delivery boys. In the process they become good friends. One boy is black and the other is white.

Why People are Different Colors, written by Julian May and illustrated by Symeon Shimin. New York: Holiday House, 1971. The story of how skin colors and hair types have changed as the human body has adapted to weather conditions. The overriding concept is that mankind is a single human species. In the forward the author writes: "An understanding of the reasons why people of many colors exist will help us to achieve genuine brotherhood among men."

Environmental Problems

The Amazing Seeds, written by Ross E. Hutchins and illustrated with photographs by the author. New York: Dodd, Mead & Co., 1960. An excellent resource for parents and teachers, and because of the superb close-up photographs, it is also suitable for young children who have not yet begun to read. Contains directions for making a seed collection.

Bits that Grow Big: Where Plants Come From, by Irma E. Webber. New York: William R. Scott, Inc., 1959. The story of man's dependency on all kinds of plants. Many excellent experiments for children to perform with growing things.

Conservation and You, by Allen S. Hitch and Marian Sorenson. Princeton, N. J.: D. Van Nostrand Co., Inc., 1964. A sobering story of how man has consistently destroyed much of his natural heritage. It presents a plea to work for conservation and preservation of the last remaining places of unspoiled nature. Included is an excellent bibliography of related readings.

Discovering Plants, written by Glenn O. Blough and illustrated by Jeanne Bendick. New York: McGraw-Hill Book Co., 1966. The author explains the function of each of a plant's parts. He shows children how to begin the process of scientific observation by using a microscope and a magnifying glass.

Ecology, The Study of Environment, written by Harold and Mary Schlichting and illustrated by Don Collins. Austin, Tex.: Steck-Vaughn Co., 1971. Young readers are introduced to the important ecological concept of the interrelationship of man, plants, and animals. The authors hope to encourage children to become amateur ecologists, and to become concerned about man's effect upon his environment.

The First Book of Trees, written by M. B. Cormack and illustrated by Helene Carter. New York: Franklin Watts, Inc., 1951. A child's introduction to trees, with excellent illustrations and scientific descriptions of the most common trees of America. Small maps show the natural range of each tree. A great deal of attention is given to products derived from the various trees and the need for replenishing forests.

The Gulf Stream, written by Ruth Brindze and illustrated by Helene Carter. New York: The Vanguard Press, 1945. The Gulf Stream is presented as a giant river flowing through the ocean, warming all the lands along its path, one of the world's greatest "weather factories."

Horned Lizards, written by M. Vere DeVault and Theodore W. Munch, illustrated by Carol Rogers. Austin, Tex.: Steck-Vaughn Co., 1957. Accurate information about horned lizards and their relatives. Large print, easy vocabulary, and colorful, detailed illustrations. Directions for making a terrarium are included. Other books in the series are: *Jackrabbits, The Armadillo, The Roadrunner,* and *The Western Diamondback Rattlesnake.*

Let's Go to Stop Water Pollution, written by Michael Chester and illustrated by Albert Micale. New York: G. P. Putnam's Sons, 1969. Told in the second person, which gives the young reader a feeling of responsibility for making rivers and bays clean again and for keeping them clean. Contains a glossary of terms related to water quality and a cross section drawing of a water treatment plant.

Life In Ponds, written by Jean Gorvett and illustrated by Paxton Chadwick. New York: American Heritage Press, 1970. This book tells children how to collect pond-water specimens and how to cultivate them for study at home or in the classroom. It shows the young scientists how to keep accurate records of their observations.

Plants in the City, written by Herman and Nina Schneider and illustrated by Cynthia Koehler, New York: The John Day Co., Inc., 1951. The story of plants in parks, yards, window boxes, florist shops, and in such unexpected places as sidewalks, rooftops and brick walls. It teaches the important concept that a plant has the ability to make its own food and what that, in turn, means to people.

Plants to Grow Indoors, written by George Sullivan and illustrated by Bill Barss. Chicago: Follett Publishing Co., 1969. An easy-to-read introduction to plant science. Thirty pages of colorfully illustrated botanical experiments that children can conduct indoors in a small space.

Secret Places, written by D. J. Arneson and photographed by Peter Arnold. New York: Holt, Rinehart & Winston, Inc., 1971. Georgous color photographs record a small boy's day of exploration in autumn woods. A shadow is cast over the boy's carefree day as he contemplates the earth-moving machinery drawing nearer and nearer to his "secret places."

Seeds and More Seeds, written by Millicent E. Selsam and illustrated by Tomi Ungerer. New York: Harper & Row, Publishers, 1959. An easy-to-read science book about seeds and plants. It shows, in story form, how a young child can plant beans and make his own seeds.

Soil, written by Richard Cromer and illustrated by Robert J. Lee. Chicago: Follett Publishing Co., 1967. An easy-to-read beginning science book. The vital importance of soil conservation is told in simple terms. Suggestions are given for easy experiments with soil and plants.

The Southern Swamps of America, written and illustrated by James R. Johnson. New York: David McKay Co., Inc., 1970. How conservation laws operate to protect an endangered species of animals by providing a wildlife refuge. Excellent resource material for parents and teachers.

What's Inside of Plants?, written by Herbert S. Zim and illustrated by Herschel Wartik. New York: William Morrow & Co., 1952. A book of botany explaining the parts and workings of familiar plants. The book is designed in such a way that pre-readers can follow the illustrations, beginning readers will be able to read the large print, and adults can read aloud the more difficult parts.

When an Animal Grows, written by Millicent E. Selsam and illustrated by John Kaufmann. New York: Harper & Row, Publishers, 1966. This is a book about the different ways newborn animals grow and are cared for by their mothers. The babies compared are a gorilla, a lamb, a duck, and a sparrow.

Your Friend, the Tree, written by Florence M. White and illustrated by Alan E. Cober. New York: Alfred A. Knopf, Inc., 1969. This book teaches children the many uses of trees and urges them to be good to trees. "When a tree is cut down, a new one should always be planted, because we cannot live without trees."

BIBLIOGRAPHY

Biber, Barbara. *Young Deprived Children and Their Educational Needs.* Washington, D. C.: Association for Childhood Education International, 1967.

Bixby, William. *A World You Can Live In: Our Ecological Past, Present, and Future.* New York: David McKay Co., Inc., 1971.

Cianciolo, Patricia Jean. "A Recommended Reading Diet for Children." *Elementary English* 48 (1971):779-787.

Coody, Betty. "Bibliotherapy: Using Books to Meet Needs." *Teaching in the 70's,* by Kenneth Briggs. Dubuque, Iowa: Kendall/Hunt Publishing Co., 1971.

Dawson, Mildred A. "Oral Interpretation." *Elementary English* 45 (1968):287-288.

Frost, Joe L., and Hawkes, Glenn R., ed. *The Disadvantaged Child, Issues and Innovations.* Boston: Houghton Mifflin Co., 1966.

Fuller, Muriel, ed. *More Junior Authors.* New York: The H. W. Wilson Co., 1963.

Gale, Raymond F. *Developmental Behavior, A Humanistic Approach.* New York: The Macmillan Co., 1969.

Georgiou, Constantine. *Children and Their Literature.* Englewood Cliffs, N. J.: Prentice-Hall, Inc., 1969.

Griffin, Louise. *Multi-Ethnic Books for Young Children.* Washington, D. C.: ERIC/NAEYC Publications, 1971.

Hoover, Kenneth H., and Hollingsworth, Paul M. *Learning and Teaching in the Elementary School.* Boston: Allyn & Bacon, Inc., 1970.

Huck, Charlotte S., and Kuhn, Doris Young. *Children's Literature in the Elementary School.* 2nd ed. New York: Holt, Rinehart & Winston, Inc., 1968.

Martin, Clyde Inez. *An Elementary School Social Studies Program.* Austin: The University of Texas Press, 1963.

Maslow, Abraham H. "A Theory of Human Motivation." *Psychological Review* 50(1943):370-396.

———. *Toward a Psychology of Being.* Princeton, N. J.: D. Van Nostrand Co., Inc., 1968.

McCoy, J. J. *Shadows Over the Land.* New York: The Seabury Press, 1970.

Meeker, Alice M. *Enjoying Literature with Children.* New York: The Odyssey Press, 1969.

Milne, A. A. *The World of Pooh.* New York: E. P. Dutton & Co., 1957.

Ozman, Howard A., Jr. "Value Implications in Children's Reading Material." *The Reading Teacher* 22 (1968):246-250.

Pfau, Donald W. "Effects of Planned Recreational Reading Programs." *The Reading Teacher* 21 (1967):35.

Smith, Henry P., and Dechant, Emerald V. *Psychology in Teaching Reading.* Englewood Cliffs, N. J.: Prentice-Hall, Inc., 1961 p. 314.

8

"Can You Suggest a Book?": Helping Parents in the Selection and Use of Children's Books

Long before a child reaches school age, his attitude and aptitude for reading have been formulated. If he has been fortunate enough to flourish and thrive in an atmosphere of language where songs rhymes, conversations, stories, and books were daily fare, his chances of success in the formal reading program are very good. To such a child, books have already brought pleasure, information, and solace; he sees them as a necessary and important part of life.

Practically speaking, the child who has grown up with books knows how to hold a book, how to turn its pages, to read left to right and top to bottom. He has a sense of the relationship between text and pictures. He is able to point out small details in illustrations, to repeat a rhythmic refrain, and to recognize the sequential development of a story. More importantly, such a child is usually able to reason, deduct and to express his thoughts in a fluent, efficient manner. In essence, he is ready to read.

A readiness to enter the school's reading program eagerly and confidently is not born out of a heavy-handed effort on the part of parents, but out of the mutual enjoyment of reading material—spontaneous, informal

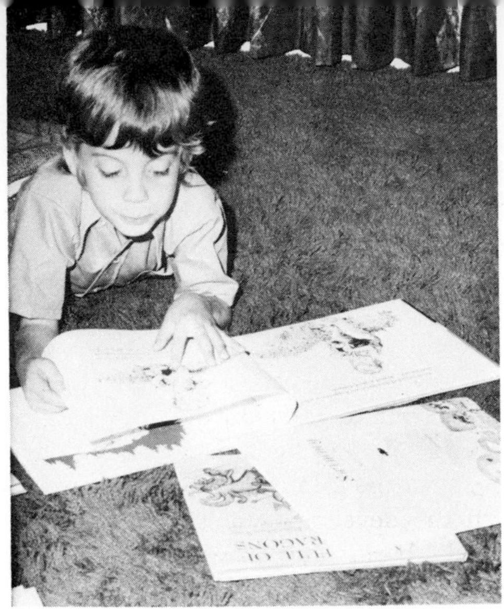

Fig. 8.1. In addition to the reading-aloud experience provided by parents, a child needs time, space, privacy, lighting, and literature for personal browsing and contemplation. (Courtesy of Pat Ryley.)

experiences with literature that were begun in infancy and continued throughout early childhood.

Well before a child celebrates his first birthday, he should be introduced to Mother Goose rhymes and to other nursery rhythms and songs by his mother and father and by other members of the family who care for him. As soon as the child begins to talk, he will repeat the sounds he has come to recognize. At first the sounds are unintelligible, but with time and practice they become more and more distinct. "The child seems to be playing with the sounds. And all the time he is learning to distinguish between sounds that are very much alike or easily confused. He is developing a sharp ear for differences. All of this will help him with his talking and later, with his reading."[1]

Once a child has matured to the point that he is willing to sit still for several minutes at a time looking at the illustrations in books, he is ready for listening to simple, brief, uncomplicated stories of the type found in picture books. *Goodnight Moon, Little Hippo, All Falling Down, Make Way for Ducklings, Play with Me, Two Lonely Ducks* and *How, Hippo!* are examples of the kind of books that might be used as "baby's first books," and they are all excellent for reading aloud as part of the ritual of bedtime.

When reading aloud to a young child, the adult should make certain that the child is in a position not only to see the pictures, but to have full access to the book. He should be allowed to help turn the pages of the book and to point out items of interest along the way. The reading should be done at a leisurely pace, with the child setting the tone, and it should

1. Nancy Larrick, *A Parent's Guide to Children's Reading* (New York: Pocket Books, 1969), p. 11.

be continued only so long as the child remains interested and attentive. Above all, the experience ought to bring pleasure to both the reader and the listener; if it fails to do so, the book should be put aside until a later date. Perhaps a different book might be needed to set matters aright.

As the reading aloud practice continues, the child enjoys having new books introduced, but he also likes to request old favorites. Some books are heard so often that he commits them to memory and is able to quote them almost verbatim. The nearer a child approaches the ability to read on his own, the more interested he becomes in the language of the book, and the more curious he becomes about the printed symbols. But because children do not proceed through the developmental stages of reading readiness at the same pace, it is risky business to generalize about them. On the other hand, if we recognize them as approximations only, some generalizations can be helpful in the study of reading readiness. The accompanying chart shows a skeleton outline of concepts that are likely to have developed when books have been used routinely with young children.[2]

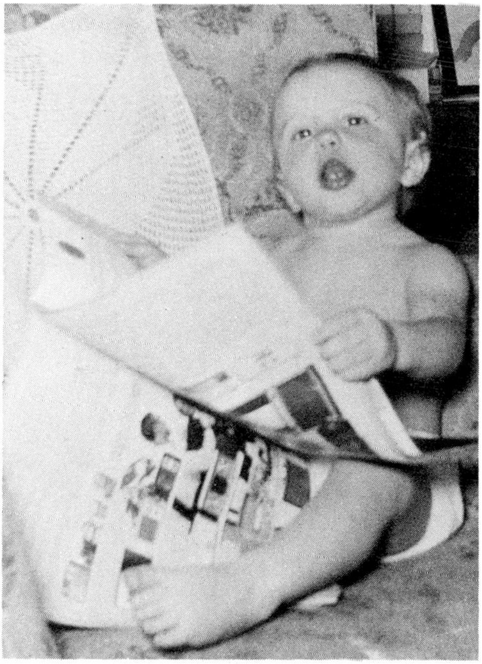

Fig. 8.2. Most infants are fascinated by newspapers, magazines, and books even before they are a year old. At this age, they enjoy the page-turning and manipulating even more than the brightly colored pictures. (Courtesy of Maydell Wilson.)

2. Chart based on information from *Foundations for Reading: Informal Pre-Reading Procedures*, by Marion Monroe and Bernice Rogers. (Glenview, Ill.: Scott, Foresman and Co., 1964), pp. 2-23. Copyright © 1964 by Scott, Foresman and Co. Reprinted by permission of the publisher.

Books and Concept Development

The First Year

Book As An Object	Books are made of interesting material. Books can be tasted, torn, manipulated.
Content of Book	Books contain brightly colored patterns. Twelve-month-old may appear to recognize realistic pictures of familiar objects.
Printed Symbols	No notice is given of printing.

From Twelve to Fifteen Months

Book As An Object	Books contain pages to be turned. Books which survive destruction may become well-loved objects.
Content of Book	Pictures resemble familiar objects. Pictures are identified in response to adult naming.
Printed Symbols	No notice is given of printing.

From Fifteen to Eighteen Months

Book As An Object	Books are to be taken care of. Tearing is usually due to lack of motor control.
Content of Book	Pictures represent objects both familiar and unfamiliar. Pictures of unfamiliar objects arouse curiosity. A few children begin to notice that pictures have a top and bottom. Pictures of familiar objects are named spontaneously. Pictures of unfamiliar objects are noticed to serve as a means of vocabulary building. Pictures are interpreted in a very simple way in terms of action or in terms of the sound the object makes.
Printed Symbols	Very rarely is notice given to printing.

From Eighteen to Twenty-four Months

Book As An Object	The child continues to develop concepts of good care of books (if care of books is taught him). He turns pages carefully and does not tear them. He realizes that the book has a front and back.
Content of Book	Pictures have a top and a bottom. Pictures do more than represent objects; they suggest action and events taking place in sequence—they tell a story. Adults tell stories about the pictures. The same language is used with reference to each picture. The events portrayed by pictures are continuous from one picture to the next. The process of looking at books is called "reading."
Printed Symbols	Two-year-olds begin to show an awareness of print—they notice that there is something else on the page besides the pictures.

From Two to Three Years

Book As An Object	Books are to be put away after use. Books are decorated with color.
Content of Book	Pictured characters often seem as real as actual people. The events pictured or told about can make one feel happy or sad or angry. Books give information one needs to know about things like trains and airplanes. The language adults use in reading books is constant for each page or picture. This language can be remembered and retold to one's self, especially if the language contains catchy sounds and jingles and is very simple and repetitive.
Printed Symbols	Some children may notice the capital letters in alphabet books, but they rarely attempt to name them.

From Three to Six Years

Book As An Object	Concepts of book care are extended. The tendency to mark in books is decreasing.
Content of Book	The language value of books now comes to the foreground and begins to rival the picture to some extent, especially if the child has good verbal ability.

Content of Book	Pictures and stories stimulate an abundant flow of ideas and expression from the child, usually of the "why" or explanatory type. The child likes to have a clear distinction made between fantasy and reality, since he is still not too sure of the difference himself. Language used in books is often memorized and repeated.
Printed Symbols	The child begins to recognize that the printed text tells the reader what to say. Print is differentiated roughly from writing. Little notice is taken of the orientation of a letter. Letters are frequently drawn or copied in reverse as well as in correct orientation.

Once parents recognize that their child's success in reading is greatly influenced by preschool experiences with literature, the problem becomes one of bringing parent and child and book together often enough to make a difference. In most modern households, this is no easy matter. Urie Bronfenbrenner writes:

> In today's world, parents find themselves at the mercy of a society which imposes pressures and priorities that allow neither time nor place for meaningful activities and relations between children and adults, which downgrade the role of parents and the functions of parenthood, and which prevent the parent from doing the things he wants to do as a guide, friend and companion to his children.[3]

Regardless of the pressures and demands of daily living, adults have a continuing responsibility to each generation of children for providing them with the many kinds of experiences necessary for normal growth and development. At the same time, they are also obligated to protect them, as much as possible, from harsh experiences that are limiting, negative, and damaging. Rudolph and Cohen point out that in spite of the busy, rushed lives of parents, various home operations and activities that take place naturally during the course of a day have the power to enrich a child's background of experiences:

> These could include errands to repair shops, really helping once in a while with cooking and cleaning or animal feeding, taking part in shopping for food, clothes and housewares, or taking a trip to the father's place of work. The mother, having the intimate relation with the child and being herself really involved in all these activities, exerts greater influence than she realizes on the preschool child's attitudes

3. Urie Bronfenbrenner, "Who Cares for America's Children?" *Young Children* (1971) vol. 15:158.

Fig. 8.3. An adult and a child share a mutual reaction to one of the illustrations in a picture book. Even a young child wants to get to the root of a matter. This natural curiosity, when encouraged and stimulated, will help the child to become a thinking, reasoning individual. (Courtesy of Michael Coody and Patricia Ryley.)

Fig. 8.4. Ideal teaching is a one-to one relationship. As this mother sings Mother Goose rhymes, the first literature of childhood, she is building for her child a firm base of language and literature. (Courtesy of H. L. Coody.)

Fig. 8.5. Nothing bridges generations and draws families together like a shared experience with literature. Here, each sister reacts to the book according to her own storehouse of experiences and her own level of understanding, but the proximity of the other girls enhances the experience. (Courtesy of Pat Russell.)

toward responsibility and toward work and workers in ethical as well as material standards.[4]

It takes an understanding teacher to assure parents of the influence that everyday home experiences exert on the lives of their children. They can be of even greater value when parents no longer take these experiences for granted but recognize them as the most powerful force in shaping the personality of a child. "Thus, during daily activities and companionship a mother is the greatest teacher to a kindergartener; she can bring much stimulation to her child if she can be helped to see where the possibilities are."[5]

Teachers must begin to look on parents as the child's first and most important teachers, and moreover, parents must begin to see themselves in this light. Certainly, there can be no justification for the wall of separation that has long existed between home and school. What young children need most are parents, teachers, and other supportive adults who will plan together, work together, and coordinate their energies into one great effort on their behalf. The following suggestions are offered as ways parents and teachers can reinforce and complement each other in providing a foundation of language and literature for young children.

How Parents Can Help

1. Create a home library for each child in the family. Enlarge the collection as he grows by adding the best books available for his age level. House them in wide shelves face out with the colorful jackets showing. Because children like owning their own titles, and are known to read more in books they own, it is well to separate their books from those belonging to older members of the family.
2. Read aloud and tell stories to young children on a day-to-day basis. If the books are carefully chosen, storytime can be enjoyable for all members of the family. The mark of a good book for young children is that it also contains characteristics appealing to older children and adults.
3. Provide a time and place for each child in the family to look at books or read in quietness and privacy. Many failures in reading have been traced to a shortage of time available in which to practice the skills of reading in self-selected materials.
4. As soon as a child is old enough to enjoy picture books, take him to the library and acquire a card in his name. Help him select books to be

4. Marguerita Rudolph and Dorothy H. Cohen, *Kindergarten, A Year of Learning* (New York: Appleton-Century-Crofts, 1964), pp. 370-371.
5. Ibid., p. 371.

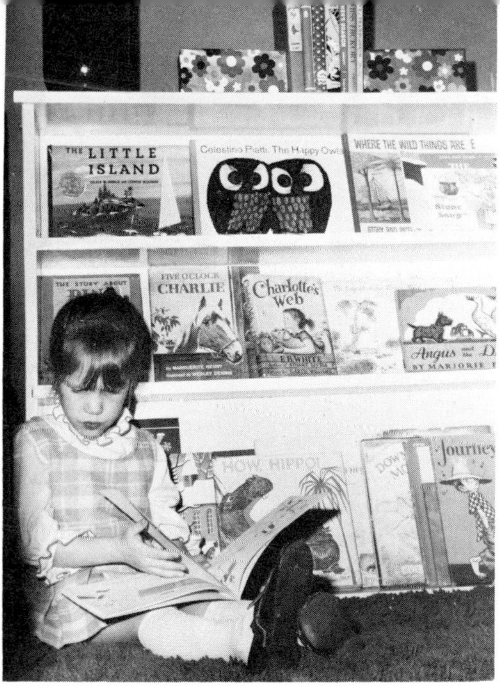

Fig. 8.6. A child's home library need not cost a fortune. Shown here is a bookcase built from scrap lumber with shelves deep enough to hold oversized books. The bookends are bricks covered with contact paper, and the reading lamp is made of a pharmacy bottle. (Courtesy of Pat Russell.)

checked out. Make each excursion to the library a pleasant experience and allow plenty of time for browsing. Lifelong attitudes toward books and readings are being formed.

5. Take advantage of bookmobile services in your community. Just going inside a bookmobile can be a memorable experience for a child. In *Tough Enough* Ruth and Latrobe Carroll describe the bookmobile's arrival at the Tatum farm:

> Once every three weeks, the bookmobile would go pushing up the road toward the Tatum farm. The Tatums and other mountain people would borrow books and keep them till the next time the bookmobile came. So it was really a little library on wheels.
>
> A librarian drove it and she also kept track of the books. The mountain people called her the book lady. She always brought her lunch in a cardboard box.[6]

6. Allow your child to accompany you to a bookstore well-stocked with children's books. A misconception is gained if a child always sees books as a sideline in a pharmacy or supermarket, and never enters a store whose sole interest is bookselling.

7. Make a study of children's books by reading as many of them as possible, and by reading the reviews of contemporary books in newspapers and magazines. Children's literature can be a fascinating hobby for adults, especially if old books and foreign books are included.

6. Ruth and Latrobe Carroll, *Tough Enough* (New York: Henry Z. Walck, Inc., 1954), p. 5.

8. Consider supplementing your child's library of hardback books with the less expensive paperbacks. Excellent books of all kinds are now being reproduced in paperback, and they are proving extremely popular with children. Write Scholastic Book Services, 904 Sylvan Ave., Englewood Cliffs, New Jersey, 07632 for information on the hundreds of paperbacks they publish for children.

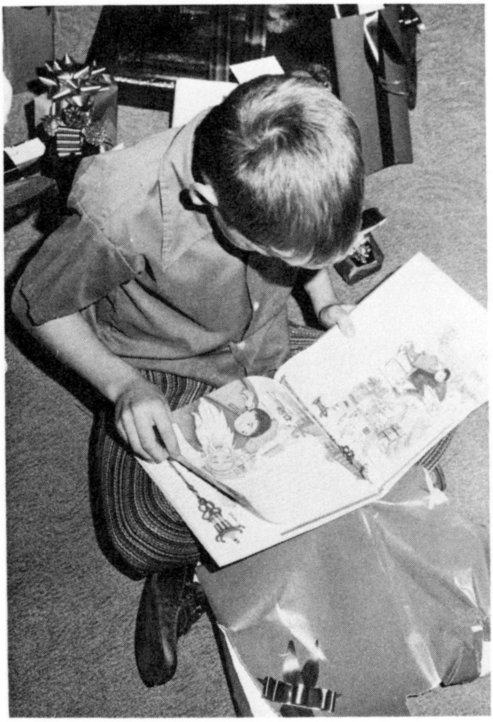

Fig. 8.7. A good book makes an enduring gift that will outlast most of the toys manufactured for children. Years later when other gifts have been forgotten, a book is remembered and cherished. (Courtesy of Josephine Shannon.)

9. Serve as an example for your child by reading newspapers, magazines, and books in his presence, and by pointing out items of interest to him from time to time. Most parents pay lip service to the value of reading, but needless to say, their actions make a greater impression.

10. Work with school officials to provide excellent central libraries for all elementary schools in your community. A statement of standards for school libraries is available from the American Library Association, 50 E. Huron St., Chicago, Illinois, 60611.

How Teachers Can Help

1. Provide parents with book lists that briefly review books of various types. The lists should include titles, authors, publishers, publication dates, and prices if they are available.

2. Instruct parents in ways to take an interest inventory in order to determine their child's preferences in reading material. Show them an informal method of ascertaining the approximate readability level of a book.

3. Make the school's professional library available to parents and encourage them to take out books on child development, reading readiness, and children's literature. Provide a simple, easy-to-use check-out system for children's books. Encourage children to take home many books that portray diverse cultures, and ways of life that are different from their own. Reading such books together can broaden the horizons of a family and further the cause of world understanding.

4. Subscribe to *Horn Book Magazine*, published six times a year by The Horn Book, Incorporated, 585 Boylston Street, Boston, Massachusetts 02116. It reviews current books for children and contains articles on children's literature. Share the magazine with interested parents.

5. Devise a record system in which each student keeps a personal account of his self-selected reading. At the semester's end, send the list or card pack home to give parents an indication of the child's achievement.

6. Under the direction of a librarian or other literature specialist, conduct a "read-in" to better acquaint parents and teachers with children's books, their authors and illustrators.

7. Draw on local college classes of speech, drama, literature, and education for storytellers, puppeteers, actors, literature specialists, and others who are able to aid in the promotion of books and reading.

8. Assist parents in surveying book club possibilities for their children. Provide names and addresses of suitable book clubs. For information on book clubs, write the Children's Book Council, 175 Fifth Avenue, New York, New York 10010. If the school purchases books for students through book clubs, explain the program to parents and enlist their cooperation.

9. Recruit parents as volunteer storytellers and library helpers. Suggest that at least one P.T.A. program each year be devoted to children's literature and reading. Enlist the help of parents in conducting a book fair. It is an excellent means of getting additional good books into the homes and classrooms of children. The Children's Book Council will provide information on book fairs.

10. Plan school-sponsored programs on children's literature for newspapers, radio, and television. Throughout such programs, continue to emphasize the role of parents in reading readiness.

11. Conduct a sidewalk art show of children's painting and sculpture inspired by their literature. Label each piece and display the book alongside.

12. Urge factories and companies to establish lending libraries of children's books for their employees to take home for reading aloud. (Most public relations men have yet to recognize this practice as a great morale booster for the entire family.)

One of the most important educational endeavors of the seventies will be the formation of parent-teacher partnerships in which young children have the security of knowing, "My parents are concerned about my education and well being, my teachers are concerned about my education and well being, and they are all in agreement about what is best for me." The most natural means of creating this bond of cooperation and esprit between home and school is a dynamic program of children's literature, with good books circulating among children, their parents and teachers. "Books that will become tattered and grimy from use, not books too handsome to grovel with. Books that will make them weep, books that will rack them with hearty laughter. Books that absorb them so that they have to be shaken loose from them. Books that they will put under the pillows at night. Books that give them gooseflesh and glimpses of glory."[7]

CHILDREN'S BOOKS FOR FAMILY ENJOYMENT

All Falling Down, written by Gene Zion and illustrated by Margaret Bloy Graham. New York: Harper & Row, Publishers, 1951. A picture book that teaches the concept of "falling down." Snow falls down, rain falls down, leaves fall down, and so do apples. An excellent book for the youngest child who will want to add many other things that fall down.

The Alphabet Tree, written and illustrated by Leo Lionni. New York: Pantheon Books, Inc., 1968. The letters of the alphabet cling to the leaves of the alphabet tree without purpose until a word bug comes along and teaches them to group themselves together into words. The purple caterpillar teaches them to group the words together into an important message for all mankind.

Another Day, written and illustrated by Marie Hall Ets. New York: The Viking Press, 1953. All the animals in the forest perform for the little boy so that he can decide which trick is best. The most unique talent of all turns out to be the little boy's ability to laugh. Excellent for the very young child.

7. Robert Lawson, "The Caldecott Medal Acceptance," *The Hornbook Magazine* 17 (1941):284.

Beanie, written and illustrated by Ruth and Latrobe Carroll. New York: Oxford University Press, 1953. Beanie is the youngest member of a large mountain-farm family of Appalachia, and the only one who does not own a pet of some kind until a birthday puppy called "Tough Enough" changes all that. The story shows warm, affectionate family relationships.

Bedtime for Frances, written by Russell Hoban and illustrated by Garth Williams. New York: Harper & Row, Publishers, 1960. Small children will recognize themselves at bedtime as Mother and Father Badger struggle to get Frances settled down to sleep on time. Beautiful, soft drawings. The badgers appear to have a furry texture.

The Big World and the Little House, written by Ruth Krauss and illustrated by Marc Simont. New York: Henry Schuman, Inc., 1949. A beautifully illustrated story of an abandoned house being transformed into a real home by a family that moves in and restores it. Throughout the book, emphasis is placed on the little house's relationship to the rest of the world, and in turn, the world's influence on the little house.

The Camel Who Took a Walk, written by Jack Tworkov and illustrated by Roger Duvoisin. New York: E. P. Dutton & Co., Inc., 1951. A brief, lively animal story filled with humor and suspense. Reminiscent of an old folk tale. Very large print.

Danny and the Dinosaur, written and illustrated by Syd Hoff. New York: Harper & Row, Publishers, 1958. An easy-to-read book about a dinosaur who leaves the museum to become Danny's friend and pet. All the children are given a ride on his back, and he learns to play hide and seek with them. At the end of a wonderful day of play he goes back to the museum, leaving Danny with memories of the fun.

Fly Homer Fly, written and illustrated by Bill Peet. Boston: Houghton Mifflin Co., 1969. A farm pigeon named Homer is lured to the big city by a sparrow named Sparky. City life is not all Homer expected it to be, and he eventually makes his way back to the farm. Sparky and the other sparrows decide Homer's is a better way of life and take up residence on the farm.

Frederick, written and illustrated by Leo Lionni. New York: Pantheon Books, Inc., 1967. While the other field mice are working to store up nuts and grain for the long hard winter, Frederick is storing up words and colors to warm them during the cold days ahead. He is such a good storyteller they are able to see the colors "as clearly as if they had them painted in their minds."

Give a Guess, written by Mary Britton Miller and illustrated by Juliet Kepes. New York: Pantheon Books, Inc., 1957. A book of riddle-poems about animals, designed to be read aloud and discussed with young children. The book presents an unusual combination of art and science.

Goodnight Moon, written by Margaret Wise Brown and illustrated by Clement Hurd. New York: Harper & Row, Publishers, 1947. A good night rhyme that names familiar objects found in a small child's room. The pages grow darker and darker toward the end of the book. Excellent as a bedtime story for infants and toddlers, and very good to foster oral language development.

A Gopher in the Garden and Other Animal Poems, written by Jack Prelutsky and illustrated by Robert Leydenfrost. New York: The Macmillan Co., 1967. Rollicking, tongue-twisting rhymes about animals of all kinds. Illustrated with humorous drawings that provide perfect accompaniment to the verses.

Hi, Mister Robin!, written by Alvin Tresselt and illustrated by Roger Duvoisin. New York: Lothrop, Lee & Shepard Co., Inc., 1950. A red-breasted robin shows a little boy how to look and listen for the unmistakable signs of spring. Very large print accompanied by beautiful paintings of spring landscapes.

Little Hippo, written by Frances Charlotte Allen and illustrated by Laura Jean Allen. New York: G. P. Putnam's Sons, 1971. After Little Hippo's mother surprises him with a baby sister, he is never lonely again. A simple and short animal story that appeals to children as young as two years of age.

Lovable Lyle, written and illustrated by Bernard Waber. Boston: Houghton Mifflin Co., 1969. Lyle the Crocodile is a favorite character of children, but in this book he finds he has an enemy. "Someone out there hates me." A mystery story with suspense and excitement for young children.

Nibble, Nibble, Poems for Children, written by Margaret Wise Brown and illustrated by Leonard Weisgard. New York: Young Scott Books, 1959. A large book of poems about plants, animals, and insects. Illustrated in the soft moss green color of nature. Suitable for children of all ages.

One Wide River to Cross, adapted by Barbara Emberley and illustrated by Ed Emberley. Englewood Cliffs, N. J.: Prentice-Hall, Inc., 1966. A famous writing-illustrating team has made use of wood block prints to illustrate this popular old folk song. The story gives children counting practice as Noah's animals come two by two, three by three, and ten by ten.

Sparky, The Story of a Little Trolley Car, written and illustrated by Hardie Gramatky. New York: G. P. Putnam's Sons, 1952. Sparky the Trolley Car's wonderful imagination livens up his routine job of running back and forth on the same track. Hardie Gramatky's stories about machines personified are always extremely popular with children.

Sung Under the Silver Umbrella, selections by the Literature Committee of the Association for Childhood Education International. New York: The Macmillan Co., 1962. One of the finest collections of poetry available for young children. Included are poems by Robert Louis Stevenson, Edna St. Vincent Millay, Christina Rossetti, and Eleanor Farjeon. The foreword was written by Padraic Colum.

Told Under the Blue Umbrella, selections by the Literature Committee of the Association for Childhood Education International and illustrated by Marguerite Davis. New York: The Macmillan Co., 1962. Short, simple stories for very young children, drawn from many sources and illustrated with black and white drawings. Excellent as a read-aloud book or as a source of tales for storytelling.

Told Under the Christmas Tree, selections by the Literature Committee of the Association for Childhood Education International and illustrated by Maud and Miska Petersham. New York: The Macmillan Co., 1948. A collection of Christmas tales and legends to tell or read aloud. Ruth Sawyer writes in the foreword: "I hope when you have finished the book you will feel as I do that the Christmas tree is a symbol of many things, shared throughout the world—a symbol of new life, of love, of laughter and of rejoicing."

Told Under the Green Umbrella, selections by the Literature Committee of the Association for Childhood Education International and illustrated by Grace

Gilkison. New York: The Macmillan Co., 1930. A collection of twenty-six of the most popular folk tales, including, "The Three Little Pigs," "The Pancake," "The Old Woman and Her Pig," and "The Straw Ox."

Told Under the Magic Umbrella, selections by the Literature Committee of the Association for Childhood Education International and illustrated by Elizabeth Orton Jones. New York: The Macmillan Co., 1939. Modern fairy tales, or "fanciful tales," as the authors label them, make up this Umbrella book. The stories portray a kind of fantasy that is present in the everyday life of a child.

Told Under Spacious Skies, selections by the Literature Committee of the Association for Childhood Education International and illustrated by William Moyers. New York: The Macmillan Co., 1952. Interesting stories about people of differing races, creeds, colors, cultures, and backgrounds, but each one an American. There was a need for this kind of book some twenty years ago when it was published, and there is still a need.

Told Under the Stars and Stripes, selections by the Literature Committee of the Association for Childhood Education International and illustrated by Nedda Walker. New York: The Macmillan Co., 1945. A collection of stories about children of many origins—Japanese-American, Mexican-American, Afro-American, American Indian and others. Such authors as Ann Nolan Clark, Marguerite de Angeli, Doris Gates, and Arna Bontemps are represented.

Two Lonely Ducks, written and illustrated by Roger Duvoisin. New York: Alfred A. Knopf, Inc., 1955. Children are given three separate counting situations in this book. They count the eggs laid by the mother duck, they count the days she sits on them, and finally they count the ducklings that hatch out.

Umbrella, written and illustrated by Taro Yashima. New York: The Viking Press, 1958. Momo's third birthday brings a new umbrella and red rubber boots, but it is many days before the rain comes. Something special happens to Momo when she carries the umbrella. Beautiful Japanese art. Excellent for reading to very young children.

Wheel on the Chimney, written by Margaret Wise Brown and illustrated by Tibor Gergely. Philadelphia, Pa.: J. B. Lippincott Co., 1954. This poetic and beautifully illustrated book follows the storks on their migratory flight to Africa and back again to their nest in a wheel on the chimney.

When Animals are Babies, written by Elizabeth and Charles Schwartz. New York: Holiday House, 1964. Realistic drawings of animal babies in their natural habitats. A comparative study of how the various baby animals eat, sleep, grow, and how they are cared for when very young.

BIBLIOGRAPHY

Bronfenbrenner, Urie. "Who Cares for America's Children?" *Young Children* 26 (1971):157-63.

Carroll, Ruth, and Carroll, Latrobe. *Tough Enough.* New York: Henry Z. Walck, Inc., 1954.

Larrick, Nancy. *A Parent's Guide to Children's Reading.* New York: Pocket Books, 1969.

Lawson, Robert. "The Caldecott Medal Acceptance." *The Hornbook Magazine* 17 (1941):273-84.
Monroe, Marion, and Rogers, Bernice. *Foundations for Reading, Informal Pre-Reading Procedures*. Glenview, Ill.: Scott, Foresman and Co., 1964.
Rudolph, Marguerita, and Cohen, Dorothy H. *Kindergarten, A Year of Learning*. New York: Appleton-Century-Crofts, 1964.

Appendix A

The Caldecott Award Book

The Caldecott medal is awarded annually by the Children's Services Division of the American Library Association. It is awarded to the artist of the most distinguished picture book for children published in the United States during the preceding year. The Caldecott medal has been awarded for the following books:

1972 *One Fine Day.* Nonny Hogrogian. Macmillan.
1971 *A Story, A Story.* Gail E. Haley. Atheneum.
1970 *Sylvester and the Magic Pebble.* William Steig. Simon & Schuster.
1969 *The Fool of the World and the Flying Ship.* Uri Shulevitz. Text by Arthur Ransome. Farrar, Strauss & Giroux.
1968 *Drummer Hoff.* Ed Emberley. Text by Barbara Emberley. Prentice-Hall.
1967 *Sam, Bangs, and Moonshine.* Evaline Ness. Holt, Rinehart & Winston.
1966 *Always Room for One More.* Nonny Hogrogian. Text by Sorche Nic Leodhas. Holt, Rinehart & Winston.
1965 *May I Bring a Friend?* Beni Montresor. Text by Beatrice Schenk de Regniers. Atheneum.
1964 *Where the Wild Things Are.* Maurice Sendak. Harper & Row.
1963 *The Snowy Day.* Ezra Jack Keats. Viking Press.
1962 *Once a Mouse . . .* Marcia Brown. Charles Scribner's Sons.

1961 *Baboushka and the Three Kings.* Nicolas Sidjakov. Text by Ruth Robbins. Parnassus Press.

1960 *Nine Days to Christmas.* Marie Hall Ets. Text by Marie Hall Ets and Aurora Labastida. Viking Press.

1959 *Chanticleer and the Fox.* Barbara Cooney. Thomas Y. Crowell.

1958 *Time of Wonder.* Robert McCloskey. Viking Press.

1957 *A Tree Is Nice.* Marc Simont. Text by Janice May Udry. Harper & Row.

1956 *Frog Went a-Courtin'.* Feodor Rojankovsky. Text by John Langstaff. Harcourt Brace Jovanovich.

1955 *Cinderella.* Marcia Brown. Text by Charles Perrault. Charles Scribner's Sons.

1954 *Madeline's Rescue.* Ludwig Bemelmans. Viking Press.

1953 *The Biggest Bear.* Lynd Ward. Houghton Mifflin.

1952 *Finders Keepers.* Nicolas Mordvinoff. Text by Will and Nicolas (Will Lipkind and Nicolas Mordvinoff). Harcourt Brace Jovanovich.

1951 *The Egg Tree.* Katherine Milhous. Charles Scribner's Sons.

1950 *Song of the Swallows.* Leo Politi. Charles Scribner's Sons.

1949 *The Big Snow.* Berta and Elmer Hader. Macmillan.

1948 *White Snow, Bright Snow.* Roger Duvoisin. Text by Alvin Tresselt. Lothrop.

1947 *The Little Island.* Leonard Weisgard. Text by Golden MacDonald (pseudo.). Doubleday.

1946 *The Rooster Crows; a Book of American Rhymes and Jingles.* Maud and Miska Petersham. Macmillan.

1945 *A Prayer for a Child.* Elizabeth Orton Jones. Text by Rachel Lyman Field. Macmillan.

1944 *Many Moons.* Louis Slobodkin. Text by James Thurber. Harcourt Brace Jovanovich.

1943 *The Little House.* Virginia Lee Burton. Houghton Mifflin.

1942 *Make Way for Ducklings.* Robert McCloskey. Viking Press.

1941 *They Were Strong and Good.* Robert Lawson. Viking Press.

1940 *Abraham Lincoln.* Ingri and Edgar Parin d'Aulaire. Doubleday.

1939 *Mei Li.* Thomas Handforth. Doubleday.

1938 *Animals of the Bible: A Picture Book.* Dorothy O. Lathrop. Text selected from the King James Bible by Helen Dean Fish. Frederick A. Stokes (Lippincott).

Appendix B

Directions for a "School-made" Incubator

1. Line a cardboard box (approximately 12″ x 12″ x 18″) with aluminum foil.
2. Line the floor of the box with cotton.
3. Cut a small opening in the lid of the box to provide a peephole for viewing and a source of ventilation.
4. Cut a hole in one side of the box near the top and insert a light socket containing a 15-watt bulb. Keep it burning at all times to maintain a temperature of 100°. As a fire precaution, be sure that the bulb does not come in contact with the box.
5. Arrange eight to twelve fertile eggs on the cotton.
6. Make an "X" on one side of each egg for easy identification in turning them.
7. Place a cup of water in one corner of the box and keep it at least one-half full at all times.
8. Sprinkle the eggs with water occasionally.
9. Gently turn the eggs once each day for the first eighteen days. The eggs should hatch on the twenty-first day.
10. When the chicks have hatched, use starter mash to feed them. Keep a light in the brooder for several days until the chicks are well established.

Note: Do not expect all of the eggs to hatch. The percentage is usually very low.

Appendix C

Publisher Index

Abelard-Schuman, Ltd., 6 W. 57th St., New York, N.Y. 10019.
Abingdon Press, 201 8th Ave., S., Nashville, Tenn. 37202.
Allyn & Bacon, Inc., 470 Atlantic Ave., Boston, Mass. 02110.
American Heritage Press, 551 5th Ave., New York, N. Y. 10017.
Appleton-Century-Crofts, 440 Park Ave., S., New York, N. Y. 10016.
Association for Childhood Education, International, 3615 Wisconsin Ave., N. W., Washington, D. C. 20016.
Blaisdell Publishing Co., Inc., 255 Wyman St., Waltham, Mass. 02154.
Brown, Wm. C. Co. Publishers, 2460 Kerper Blvd., Dubuque, Iowa 52001.
Columbia University Press, 440 W. 110th St., New York, N. Y. 10026.
Coward-McCann, Inc., 200 Madison Ave., New York, N. Y. 10016.
Day, The John Co., 62 West 45th St., New York, N. Y. 10036.
Denison, T. S. & Co., Inc., 315 5th Ave., S., Minneapolis, Minn. 55415.
Dial Press, 750 3rd Ave., New York, N. Y. 10017.
Dodd, Mead & Co., 79 Madison Ave., New York, N. Y. 10016.
Doubleday & Co., Inc., 277 Park Ave., New York, N. Y. 10017.
Dover Publications, Inc., 180 Varick St., New York, N. Y. 10014.
Dutton, E. P. & Co., Inc., 201 Park Ave., S., New York, N. Y. 10003.
Follett Publishing Co., 1010 W. Washington Blvd., Chicago, Ill. 60607.
Golden Press, Inc., 850 Third Ave., New York, N. Y. 10022.
Harcourt Brace Jovanovich, 757 Third Ave., New York, N. Y. 10017.
Harper & Row, Publishers, 49 E. 33rd St., New York, N. Y. 10016.
Heath, D. C. & Co., 285 Columbus Ave., Boston, Mass. 02116.
Holiday House, 18 E. 56th St., New York, N. Y. 10022.

Holt, Rinehart & Winston, Inc., 383 Madison Ave., New York, N. Y. 10017.

Horn Book, Inc., 585 Boylston St., Boston, Mass. 02116.

Houghton Mifflin Co., 53 W. 43rd St., New York, N. Y. 10036.

Indiana University Press, 10th & Morton Sts., Bloomington, Ind. 47401.

Kendall/Hunt Publishing Co., 2460 Kerper Blvd., Dubuque, Iowa 52001.

Knopf, Alfred A., Inc., 501 Madison Ave., New York, N. Y. 10022.

Lane Magazine and Book Co., Menlo Park, Calif. 94025.

Lippincott, J. B. Co., E. Washington Sq., Philadelphia, Pa. 19105.

Little, Brown & Co., 34 Beacon St., Boston, Mass. 02106.

Lothrop, Lee & Shephard Co., 419 Park Ave., S., New York, N. Y. 10016.

Macmillan Co., The, 866 Third Ave., New York, N. Y. 10022.

McKay, David Co., Inc., 750 Third Ave., New York, N. Y. 10017.

McGraw-Hill Book Co., 330 W. 42nd St., New York, N. Y. 10036.

Merrill, Charles E. Books, Inc., College Div., 1300 Alum Creek Dr., Columbus, Ohio 43216.

Morrow, William and Co., 425 Park Ave., S., New York, N. Y. 10016.

National Council of Teachers of English, 508 S. Sixth St., Champaign, Ill. 61820.

New American Library, Inc., 1301 Ave. of the Americas, New York, N. Y. 10019.

Odyssey Press, Inc., 55 5th Ave., New York, N. Y. 10003.

Oxford University Press, Inc., 200 Madison Ave., New York, N. Y. 10016. Orders to 1600 Pollitte Drive, Fair Lawn, N. J. 07410.

Pantheon Books, Inc., 22 E. 51st St., New York, N. Y. 10022.

Parents Magazine Press, 52 Vanderbilt Ave., New York, N. Y. 10017.

Pocket Books, 1 W. 39th St., New York, N. Y. 10018.

Prentice-Hall, Inc., 70 5th Ave., New York, N. Y. 10011.

Putnam's, G. P. Sons, 200 Madison Ave., New York, N. Y. 10016.

Scarecrow Press, Inc., 52 Liberty St., Box 656, Metuchen, N. J. 08840.

Scholastic Book Services, 50 W. 44th St., New York, N. Y. 10036.

Scott, Foresman and Co., 1900 E. Lake Ave., Glenview, Ill. 60025.

Scott, William R., Inc., 333 Ave. of the Americas, New York, N. Y. 10014.

Scribner's, Charles Sons, 597 Fifth Ave., New York, N. Y. 10017.

Steck-Vaughn Co., Box 2028, Austin, Texas 78761.

Tuttle, Charles E. Co., 28 S. Main St., Rutland, Vt. 05701.

University of Texas Press, Austin, Texas 78712.

Vanguard Press, 424 Madison Ave., New York, N. Y. 10017.

Van Nostrand Co., Inc., Princeton, N. J. 08540.

Viking Press, Inc., 625 Madison Ave., New York, N. Y. 10022.

Walck, Henry Z., Inc., 19 Union Sq., W., New York, N. Y. 10003.

Watts, Franklin, Inc., 575 Lexington Ave., New York, N. Y. 10022.

Wilson, H. W. Co., 950 University Ave., Bronx, N. Y. 10452.

Index

ABC, An Alphabet Book, 16
ABC Bunny, The, 16
A,B,C, Go!, 56
Adventures of Three Colors, The, 17
Aesop's Fables, 90, 93
All About Eggs and How They Change Into Animals, 79
All Falling Down, 145, 154
Allen, Frances Charlotte, 156
Allen, Laura Jean, 156
Allen, R. V., 64, 67
Alligators All Around, 86, 93
Almy, Millie Corrine, 61
Alphabet books, 4
Alphabet Tree, The, 154
Amazing Seeds, The, 139
Amelia Bedelia, 78
American Library Association, The Children's Services Division of, 6, 52, 91
Amigo, 19
Anatole and the Cat, 47, 57
An Elementary School Social Studies Program, 136
Anglund, Joan Walsh, 16
Angus and the Ducks, 87, 93
Animals of the Bible, 91
Animal Stories, 5
Another Day, 154
Applesauce, recipe for, 123
Apt, 3, 134, 138
Arbuthnot, Mae Hill, 23
Ardizzone, Edward, 47, 58
Are You My Mother? 19
Armadillo, 140
Arneson, D. J., 140
Arno, Ed, 111
Arnold, Peter, 140
Art, 103, 105, 106, 108, 110, 111, 114, 116, 119, 121, 122, 124, 126
Art experiences
  books that lead to, 82, 93
  in children's books, 90
Art of the Puppet, The, 47
Art of the Story-Teller, The, 26
Ask Mr. Bear, 134, 137
Association for Childhood Education International, Literature Committee of the, 156, 157
Atwater, Florence, 94
Atwater, Richard, 94
Audiovisual aids, 62

Baby Sister for Frances, A, 89, 93
Bailey, Carolyn Sherwin, 18, 22, 39, 40, 80
Baird, Bil, 47
Barss, Bill, 140
Basic needs of early childhood, 131
Batchelder, Marjorie, 47
Beanie, 155

Bears on Hemlock Mountain, The, 47, 57
Bedford, Annie North, 125
Bedtime for Frances, 155
Beim, Jerrold, 139
Beim, Lorraine, 139
Believe and Make-Believe, 35
Belting, Natalia M., 40
Bendick, Jeanne, 139
Benjie on His Own, 135, 137
Bennett, Rainey, 18
Bernard, Harold W., 64
Beskow, Elsa, 80
Biber, Barbara, 132
Bibliotherapy, 7, 127
  children's books for, 137
Big Snow, The, 85, 93
Big World and the Little House, The, 155
Bileck, Marvin, 19
Bits that Grow Big: Where Plants Come From, 139
Blackberry jam, recipe for, 107
Black, Irma Simonton, 35
Blough, Glenn O., 139
Blueberries for Sal, 14, 103, 104
Blueberry Cupcakes, recipe for, 103
Book of Myths, 90, 93
Book of Nursery and Mother Goose Rhymes, 15
Book
  parts of a, 14
  people who make a, 13
Books
  check-out system of, 8
  displays of, 7
  made by children, 12
  self-selection of, 3
  special categories, 8
Bowen, Mary E., 76
Bradbury, Ray, 95
Bread and Jam for Frances, 106-7
"Bremen Town Musicians," 50
Brewster, Benjamin, 57
Briggs, Kenneth, 127
Brindze, Ruth, 140
Brittain, W. Lambert, 76
Bronfenbrenner, Urie, 148
Brooke, Leslie, 94
Brown, Marcia, 16, 18, 19, 23, 29, 47, 58, 92, 95, 116, 137
Brown, Margaret Wise, 155, 156, 157
Bryant, Al, 40
Buck, Pearl S., 40
Bulletin boards, 6
Burrows, Alvina Treut
Burton, Virginia Lee, 17, 94
Burton, William H., 64, 83

Caldecott Award, The, 6, 78, 91, 92, 121, 122, 124
Caldecott Medal Acceptance, The, 154
Caldecott, Randolph, 91
Camel Who Took a Walk, 155
Caps for Sale, 86, 93
Carroll, Latrobe, 151, 155
Carroll, Ruth, 151, 155
Carrots, recipe for buttered, 119
Carrot Seed, The, 119, 120
Carter, Helene, 140
Chadwick, Paxton, 140
Chambellan, René Paul, 91
Chambers, Dewey W., 25
Charlotte's Web, 87, 93, 127
Chart making, 70
"Cheese, Peas, and Chocolate Pudding," 35
Chester, Michael, 140
Chicken Soup with Rice, 105
Chicken soup with rice, recipe for, 105
Child development, 61
Children and Books, 23
Children and Their Literature, 135
Children and the Language Arts, 3
Children's Book Council, 153
"Children's Experiences in Literature," 3
"Children's Experiences Prior to First Grade and Success in Beginning Reading," 61
Children's Literature for Dramatization: An Anthology, 557
Children's Literature in the Elementary School, 128
Children's Literature: Strategies of Teaching, 45

Chimney Corner Stories, 57
Chwast, Seymour, 16
Cianciolo, Patricia Jean, 130
"Cinderella," 19, 23, 50, 90
Clark, Ann Nolan, 138
Clark, Margery, 101
Cleaver, Nancy, 94
Cober, Alan E., 141
Cohen, Dorothy H., 43, 150
Collage, 87
Collins, Don, 140
Colum, Padraic, 23, 24, 25
Concept development, 146
Contributions to Reading, 61
Controlled vocabulary, 6
Conservation and You, 139
Coody, Betty, 127
Cooking experiences, books that lead to, 97
Cormack, M. B., 140
Cow Who Fell in the Canal, The, 77, 79
Creative and Mental Growth, 76
Creative dramatics, 43, 46
Creative Teaching in the Elementary School, 2
Creative writing, 75
  literature and, 78
  the teacher of, 76
Creativity, 15
"Creativity in the Very Young," 83
Creativity: Its Educational Implications, 83
Credle, Ellis, 79, 132
Crews, Donald, 17
Crichlow, Ernest, 139
Crictor, 18
Cromer, Richard, 141
Cross-age grouping, 92
Crow Boy, 19, 133, 135
Crows of Pear Blossom, The, 69
Curious George, 17

Daddies, What They Do All Day, 89
Dalgliesh, Alice, 47, 57, 108
Danny and the Dinosaur, 155
Davis, Marguerite, 156
Dawson, Mildred A., 137
de Angeli, Marguerite, 15, 138
de Brunhoff, Laurent, 95
Dechant, Emerald V., 65, 129
Demos, George D., 83
Dennis, Wesley, 79
de Regniers, Beatrice Schenk, 47, 58
Developmental Behavior, A Developmental Approach, 134
DeVault, M. Vere, 140
Dewey, John, 64
Disadvantaged Child, Issues and Innovations, The, 132
Discovering Plants, 139
Discussion, follow-up to story, 11
Dobbs, Rose, 58
Dodge, Dick, 139
Dolezal, Carroll, 95
Down, Down the Mountain, 78, 79, 132
Dramatic play, 43
Dramatization, literature for, 42, 56
Drummer Hoff, 47, 57
Duchess Bakes a Cake, The, 110
Duvoisin, Roger, 57, 94, 95, 124, 155, 156, 157

Early Childhood Education Rediscovered, 65
Easel Painting, 89
Easter eggs, recipe for, 121
Eastman, P. D., 19
Easy-to-read books, 6
Ecology, The Study of Environment, 140
Education for Effective Thinking, 64
"Effects of Planned Recreational Reading Programs," 130
Egg Tree, The, 121, 122
Elementary English, 22, 23, 130, 137
"Elephant's Child, The," 77
Emberley, Barbara, 47, 57, 156
Emberley, Ed, 57, 156
English Language Arts, The, 63
Enjoying Literature with Children, 130
Ets, Marie Hall, 47, 58, 138, 154
Evans, Pauline Rush, 57
Experience and Education, 64
Experience charts, 65
  composing, 67

illustrating, 71
sources of, 67
uses of, 67, 72, 73, 74

Family Treasury of Children's Stories, 57
Fatio, Louise, 47, 57
Favorite Stories for the Children's Hour, 39
Felice, 137
Field, Rachel, 79
Finders Keepers, 47, 57
First ABC, 16
First Book of Trees, The, 140
First Book of Indians, The, 57
"Fisherman and His Wife, The," 28
Five Chinese Brothers, The, 69
500 Hats of Bartholomew Cubbins, The, 86, 93
Five O'Clock Charlie, 77, 79
Flack, Marjorie, 93, 95, 137, 139
Flannelboard Stories for the Primary Grades, 37
Fly Homer Fly, 155
Folk literature, 21
rhymes, 4
tales, 22, 24
Foundations for Reading: Informal Pre-Reading Procedures, 145
Françoise, 47, 58
Frederick, 155
Frieze construction, 85
Friskey, Margaret, 47, 59
Frost, Joe L., 65, 132
Frosty, the Snowman, 125
Fuller, Muriel, 133

Gág, Wanda, 16, 18, 40
Gale, Raymond F., 134
Gannett, Ruth Chrisman, 80
Gannett, Ruth Stiles, 80
Gekiere, Madeline, 95
Georgiou, Constantine, 135
Gergely, Tibor, 157
Gilberto and the Wind, 138
Gilkison, Grace, 157
Gingerbread Boy, The, 89
Gingerbread Man, The, 111, 114, 115
Gingerbread Men, recipe for, 111
Give a Guess, 155
Glanzman, Louis S., 80
Goodnight Moon, 145, 155
Gopher in the Garden and Other Animal Poems, A, 155
Gorvett, Jean, 140
Gowan, John Curtis, 83
Grade Teacher, 77
Graham, Margaret Bloy, 17, 154
Gramatky, Hardie, 17, 156
Green, Milton, 16
Grimm, Jacob, 28
Grimm, Wilhelm, 28
Gulf Stream, The, 140

Hader Berta, 93
Hailstones and Halibut Bones, 89, 94
"Hansel and Gretel," 51
Happy Lion, The, 47, 57
Happy Owls, The, 19, 85
Harris, Ben M., 61
Harry the Dirty Dog, 17, 77
Hawkes, Glenn R., 132
Health and safety, 99, 104, 106, 107, 109, 111, 114, 117, 119, 120, 122, 126
Heffernan, Helen, 83
Heilman, Arthur W., 72
"Henny Penny," 50
Henry-Fisherman, 47, 58
Henry, Marguerite, 79
Herrera, Velino, 138
Herrick, Virgil E., 4
Hitty, Her First Hundred Years, 78
Hi, Mister Robin, 156
Hints to the Teacher, 100
Hitch, Allen S., 139
Hoban, Lillian, 93, 107
Hoban, Russell, 93, 107, 155
Hoff, Syd, 138, 155
Hogrogian, Nonny, 139
Hollingsworth, Paul M., 135
Homer Price, 78, 79
Hoover, Kenneth H., 135
Horn Book Magazine, 153, 154
Horned Lizards, 140
Horton Hatches the Egg, 18
How Hippo!, 18, 92, 145
Huchins, Ross E., 139
Huck, Charlotte S., 128

Humor and nonsense books, 6
Hundred Dresses, The, 134
Hurd, Clement, 155
Hutchinson, Veronica S., 57

Illustrations, 4
Illustrators, 13
In My Mother's House, 138

Jablow, Alta, 40
"Jack and the Beanstalk," 50
Jackrabbits, 140
Jacobi, Frederick, Jr., 40
Jacobs, Leland, 3
Jeanne-Marie Counts Her Sheep, 47, 58
Johnnycake, 114
Johnny Crow's Garden, 18, 89, 94
Johnson, James R., 141
Jones, Elizabeth Orton, 157
Journey Cake Ho!, 114, 115
Journey cake, recipe for, 115
Juanita, 138
Just So Stories, 77, 80

Kahl, Virginia, 110
Karaz, Ilonka, 16
Kaufman, John, 141
Keats, Ezra Jack, 125, 138
Keller, Helen, 66
Kepes, Juliet, 155
Kimball, Roland B., 64
Kindergarten, A Year of Learning, 43
Kipling, Rudyard, 80
Kirkton, Carole Mosley, 22
Koehler, Cynthia, 140
Koering, Ursula, 57
Kohl, Herbert, 77
Kramer, Nora, 58
Krasilovsky, Phyllis, 79
Krauss, Ruth, 119, 155
Kuhn, Doris Young, 128
Krush, Beth, 58
Krush, Joe, 58

Lamoreaux, Lillian A., 60
Language Arts, 101, 104, 105, 107, 108, 110, 112, 115, 117, 118, 120, 121, 123, 124
Language Arts in Elementary Schools, 62
Language Experience, 60
  books and the, 69
  books for, 79
Language Skills in Elementary Education, 35
Larrick, Nancy, 16, 82, 145
Lathrop, Dorothy P., 79, 91
Lawson, Robert, 94, 154
Leaf, Munro, 18
Learning and Teaching in the Elementary School, 135
Learning centers, 43
Learning to Read Through Experience, 60, 64
Lee, Dorris May, 60, 64, 67
Lee, Robert J., 141
Legend of the Willow Plate, The, 90, 94
Lenski, Lois, 57, 94
Leonni, Leo, 95, 154, 155
Let's Go to Stop Water Pollution, 140
Lewis, Clara M., 39
Lewis, Shari, 48
Lexau, Joan, 137
Leydenfrost, Robert, 155
Librarians, children as, 7
Library center, the, 6
Life in ponds, 140
Lindgren, Astrid, 80
Lindman, Maj, 11
Lipkind, Will, 47, 57
Literature for Children: Storytelling and Creative Drama, 25
Little Airplane, The, 94
Little Auto, The, 89, 94
Little Bear's Visit, 19
Little Chief, 134, 138
Little Engine that Could, The, 17, 135
Little Fire Engine, The, 94
Little Hippo, 145, 156
Little House, The, 85, 94
Little Island, The, 19, 85
Little Rabbit Who Wanted Red Wings, The, 18
"Little Red Hen and the Grain of Wheat, The," 50

"Little Red Riding Hood," 50
Little Tim and the Brave Sea Captain, 47, 58
Little Toot, 17
Little Toot on the Thames, 17
Little Train, The, 94
Lovable Lyle, 156
Lowenfield, Viktor, 76
Low, Joseph, 94
Ludwig, Helen, 79

Machines Personified, 5
Make Way for Ducklings, 87, 92, 94, 145
Making Easy Puppets, 48
Man in the Moon, The, 40
Many Moons, 69, 80
Marcel Marceau Alphabet Book, The, 16
"Marcia Brown: A Study in Versatility," 23
Martignoni, Margaret E., 56
Martin, Clyde Inez, 136
Maslow, Abraham H., 128, 132
Mathematics, 102, 104, 106, 107, 109, 111, 114, 115, 117, 119, 120, 122, 123, 126
Mathon, Laura E., 40
Mathiesen, Thomas, 16
Mattil, Edward L., 19, 49
May I Bring A Friend? 47, 58
Meaning in Crafts, 49
Meeker, Alice M., 130
Mendoza, George, 16
Merry Tales for Children, 40
Micale, Albert, 140
Milhous, Katherine, 121
Mike Mulligan and His Steam Shovel, 17
Miller, Mary Britton, 155
Millions of Cats, 18, 86
Milne, A. A., 137
Milner, Esther, 61
Minarik, Else Holmelund, 19
Miss Hickory, 78, 80
Mitchell, Lucy Sprague, 35
Moffett, James, 5
Monroe, Marion, 145
Montage, 89
Moore, Lilian, 16
Mordvinoff, Nicholas, 47, 57
More Junior Authors, 133
More Tales from Grimm, 40
Morey, Jean, 59
Mosaic, 88
Moskof, Martin Stephens, 16
Mother Goose, 4, 15, 144
Moyers, William, 157
"Mr. and Mrs. Vinegar," 50
Mr. Penny, 47, 58
Mr. Popper's Penguins, 86, 94
Mr. Rabbit and the Lovely Present, 89
Munch, Theodore, W., 140
Mural Making, 84
Music, 114
My Father's Dragon, 78, 80
My First Counting Book, 16
McCloskey, Robert, 14, 19, 79, 90, 94, 95, 103, 105, 114

Nail Soup, 117, 118
Nail Soup, recipe for, 118
Nannabah's Friend, 138
National Council of Teachers of English, 63
Need for Change, 6
Needs
  esteem, 134
  for self-actualization, 135
  love and belonging, 133
  physiological, 132
  safety, 132
New Pet, The, 139
Nibble, Nibble, Poems for Children, 156
Nora Kramer's Storybook, 58
Nutshell Library, 105

"Old Woman and Her Pig, The," 51
Once a Mouse, 92
Once Upon a Time, 58
"Once upon . . . Folk Tales and Storytelling," 22
1 is One, 17
One Morning in Maine, 104
O'Neill, Marg, 94
One–Two–Three–Four Cake, recipe for, 110
One Wide River to Cross, 156

Oral interpretation, 137
Ozman, Howard A., 129

Painter, Helen W., 23
Pancake, The, 50, 114, 115
Pantomime, 43, 45
Parents, conferences with, 8, 143
Parents Guide to Children's Reading, A, 145
Paz, 139
Peet, Bill, 155
Pelle's New Suit, 80, 135
Pennsylvania Dutch designs, 122
Perrine, Mary, 138
Personality development, 2
Peter Piper's Alphabet, 16
Peter's Chair, 89
Petersham, Maud, 101, 156
Petersham, Miska, 101, 156
Petty, Walter T., 76
Petunia, 89, 94
Petunia and the Song, 94
Petunia Takes a Trip, 94
Pfau, Donald W., 130
Piatti, Celestino, 19
Picture books, 6, 91
Pied Piper of Hamelin, The, 78
Piper, Watty, 17
Pippi Longstocking, 78, 80
Plants in the City, 140
Plants to Grow Indoors, 140
Play With Me, 58, 145
Poetry, 77
Politi, Leo, 138
Poppy Seed Cakes, The, 101, 102
Poppy Seed Cakes, recipe for, 101
Potter, Beatrix, 95
Prelutsky, Jack, 155
Principles and Practices of Teaching Reading, 72
"Prop" boxes, 44
Provenson, Alice, 93
Provenson, Martin, 93
Psychological Review, 132
Psychology in Teaching Reading, 65, 129
Psychology of Learning and Teaching, 64
Publisher, 13
Pucci, Albert John, 138
Pumpkin pies, recipe for, 108-9
Puppet construction
  box puppets, 53
  cylinder puppets, 53
  fruit and vegetable, 53
  humanette, 56
  mask puppets, 56
  paper sack, 52
  rubber ball, 52
  shadow puppets, 53
  sock puppets, 52
  stick puppets, 53
Puppetry, 43, 47
Puppet Theatre Handbook, The, 48
Puppet types
  hand, 51
  marionette, 51
  rod, 51
  shadow, 51

"Queer Company," 37
Questioning Methods, 11
Question types, 11

Rabbit Hill, 87, 94
Rain Makes Applesauce, 18, 122
Readability level, 6
Reading
  achievement, 7
  aloud, 1, 9, 145
  attitude toward, 1
  failure in, 1, 60
  interest in, 4
  programs, 1
  readiness, 1, 70, 143
Reading records
  for children, 8
  for teachers, 8
Reading Teacher, The, 129, 130
Real Mother Goose, The, 15
Recipe Charts, 98
Recipes, 98
"Recommended Reading Diet for Children, A," 130
Rey, Hans A., 17
Roadrunner, 140
Robuck, Mildred C., 83
Rogers, Bernice, 145
Rogers, Carol, 140
Rojankovsky, Feodor, 15

Rudolph, Marguerita, 43, 150
"Rumpelstiltskin," 51
Ryan, Cheli Duran, 139

Safety, 116
Sawyer, Ruth, 26, 115
Schaer, Julian, 123
Schlichting, Harold, 140
Schlichting, Mary, 140
Schmidt, Thusnelda, 40
Schneider, Herman, 140
Schneider, Nina, 140
Scholastic Book Services, 152
Schwartz, Charles, 157
Schwartz, Elizabeth, 157
Schweitzer, Byrd Baylor, 19
Science, 102, 104, 106, 107, 109, 111, 114, 115, 117, 119, 120, 122, 123, 126
Secret Hiding Place, 18
Secret Places, 140
Self-selection, 84
Selsam, Millicent, 79, 141
Sendak, Maurice, 93, 105
Seeds and More Seeds, 141
Seuss, Dr. (Theodore Seuss Geisel), 18, 93
Seven Diving Ducks, 47, 59
Sewell, Helen, 93
Shawnee Cake, 115
Shedlock, Marie L., 26
Sheer, Julian, 18
Shumsky, Abraham, 2
Sibley, Donald, 57
Siks, Geraldine Brain, 57
Simont, Marc, 155
Sky Full of Dragons, A., 86, 95
Slithery Snakes and other Aids to Children's Writing, 76
Slobodkina, Esphyr, 93
Slobodkin, Louis, 80
Smith, Henry P., 65, 129
Snip, Snapp, Snurr and the Red Shoes, 11
Snowman Cake, recipe for, 124
"Snow White," 23
Snowy Day, The, 125
Social Science, 102, 104, 106, 107, 108, 109, 111, 114, 115, 117, 118, 120, 122, 123, 125
Soil, 141
Sorenson, Marian, 39
Southern Swamps of America, The, 141
Sparky, The Story of a Little Trolley Car, 156
Spier, Peter, 79
Steig, William, 19
Step Beyond: Creativity, The, 83
Still Another Number Book, 16
Stone Soup, 116
Stone Soup, recipe for, 116
Stories for Little Children, 40
Stories to Tell Boys and Girls, 40
Storytelling, 21, 26
  preparing the story, 28
  selecting the story, 26
Story About Ping, The, 95
Story of Babar, The, 87, 95
Story of Ferdinand, The, 18, 87
Story of My Life, The, 66
Storyteller, The, 25
Storytelling
  aids to, 30, 35
  barriers to, 34
  creating a climate, 29
  time for, 31
  value of, 27
Storytelling Hour, The, 22
Storytelling New and Old, 23
Story Well, 31
Strickland, Ruth G., 62
Student-Centered Language Arts Curriculum, A, Grades K-12: Handbook for Teachers, 5
"Study of the Relationship Between Reading Readiness in Grade One School Children and Patterns of Parent-Child Interactions, A," 61
Sun is a Golden Earring, The, 40
Sung Under the Silver Umbrella, 156
Sullivan, George, 40
Supervisory Behavior in Education, 61
Swimming, 89, 95
Switch on the Night, 85, 95
Sylvester and the Magic Pebble, 19
Symeon, Shimin, 139

Tale of Peter Rabbitt, The, 89, 95
Tales from Grimm, 28, 40
Tales of Grimm and Anderson, 40
Tall Book of Mother Goose, The, 15
Taylor, Talus, 17
Teacher Aide, 69, 71
Teachers Guide to Children's Books, A, 82
Teaching in the 70's, 127
Teaching for Creative Endeavor, 83
Tenggren, Gustaf, 15
Tengren Mother Goose, The, 15
Thanksgiving Story, The, 108
Theodore Turtle, 87
Theory of Human Motivation, A, 132
They All Want to Write, 75
"Three Bears, The," 50
"Three Billy Goats Gruff," 23, 29, 50, 90, 95, 108
Three Gay Tales from Grimm, 40
"Three Little Kittens, The," 50
"Three Little Pigs, The," 23, 50
Thurber, James, 80
Time of Wonder, 85, 92, 95
Tison, Annette, 17
Titus, Eve, 47, 57
Told Under the Blue Umbrella, 156
Told Under the Christmas Tree, 156
Told Under the Green Umbrella, 156
Told Under the Magic Umbrella, 156
Told Under Spacious Skies, 157
Told Under the Stars and Stripes, 157
Too Many Sisters, 139
Tooze, Ruth, 26
Torrance, E. Paul, 15, 83
Tough Enough, 151
Toward a Psychology of Being, 128
Trauger, Wilma K., 62
Treasured Tales, 40
Tree Is Nice, A, 85, 95
Tresselt, Alvin, 94, 124, 156
Tudor, Tasha, 15, 17
Two Is a Team, 139
Two Lovely Ducks, 145, 157
The Twelve Days of Christmas, 16
Tworkov, Jack, 155

Udry, Janice May, 95
Umbrella, 157
Ungerer, Tomi, 18, 141
Untermeyer, Louis, 40

"Value Implications in Children's Reading," 129
Vance, Eleanor Graham, 138
Veronica, 89, 95

Waber, Bernard, 156
Walker, Nedda, 157
Wartik, Herschel, 141
Way of the Storyteller, The, 26
Webber, Irma, E., 139
We Read A to Z, 17
Weisgard, Leonard, 19, 94, 138, 156
Western Diamondback Rattlesnake, The, 140
What's Inside of Plants?, 141
Wheel on the Chimney, 157
When an Animal Grows, 141
Where the Wild Things Are, 69
Whistle for Willie, 135, 138
White, E. B., 93
White, Florence M., 141
Whitehead, Robert, 45, 46
White Snow Bright Snow, 124, 126, 134
"Who Cares for America's Children?" 148
Why People Are Different Colors, 139
Wiese, Kurt, 95
Wigg, Richard L., 64
Wilson, John A. R., 83
Williams, Garth, 16, 19, 93, 155
Withers, Carl, 40
Witsen, Betty Van, 35
Wright, Mildred Whatley, 95
"Writing Their Way to Self-Acceptance," 77
"Wolf and the Seven Little Kids, The," 51
World of Pooh, The, 173
World's Great Stories: 55 Legends that Live Forever, The, 40

Yashima, Taro, 19, 133, 157
Yonie Wondernose, 135, 138
Young Children, 148

Young Deprived Children and Their Educational Needs, 132
Your Friend the Tree, 141
Zemach, Harve, 117
Zim, Herbert, 141
Zion, Gene, 17, 154